FIERCE

Fierce

The Power of Owning Your Journey

AMBER ADAMS-DIXON-CAMPBELL

Fierce: The Power of Owning Your Journey

yourfiercestrategy@gmail.com

Published by:

Grow Rich Publishing

204-236 2nd Street West

North Vancouver, BC

V7M 1C6

Limits of Liability and Disclaimer

This book is strictly for informational and educational purposes only and is not intended to be a substitute for seeking personalized, professional advice. The author and/or publisher do not guarantee that anyone following these techniques, suggestions, tips, ideas, or strategies will become successful. The author and/or publisher shall have neither liability nor responsibility to anyone with respect to any loss or damage caused, or alleged to be caused, directly or indirectly by the information contained in this book.

ISBN: 978-1-990185-00-7

Dedication

For every individual told they can't, they won't, and they shouldn't -
YOU are my *FIERCE* warriors and
your time is NOW!

For Grace, Grant, & Dylan this journey is yours
and yours alone and I will always be with you as a reminder
you can dream big and be *FIERCE!*

Table of Contents

Fierce

"It's not what you say to everyone else that determines your life; it's what you whisper to yourself that has the greatest power"

— marc & angel

Congratulations on taking the first step in owning your *FIERCE* journey! What does it mean to be *Fierce*? Do you imagine a lion or lioness when you think of the word? How about a celebrity like Beyoncé or a historical figure like Martin Luther King Jr.? Maybe it's someone you know like a mentor, coach, or parent? How often when you hear the word *Fierce* do you think of yourself? Animals can be fierce – aggressive, ferocious, savage. Storms can be fierce – powerful, strong, violent. But what about us? Can we be fierce as humans? Can we also have a level of intensity and strength that exudes from our pores?

It is my belief that we can be fierce in everything we do. Fiercely ambitious, fiercely loyal, fiercely kind, fiercely loving, and fiercely intentional about all that we say and do with our time on this earth. If we set out to be intentional with our lives then it is not left up to chance, to the wind, or to the external world to decide for us. Being fierce comes with a level of self-respect and self-love that means that not only do you know yourself, your limit's and capabilities, but that you also possess the inner strength to weather any storm. Having confidence and determination are certain qualities of *Fierce* that many of us associate with people who we associate with this word. However, I would challenge us to see beyond the dictionary definition and broaden our view.

Fierce is to be intimately aware of one's purpose, values, strengths, and dreams such that the journey is filled with an intense passion for life.

Being fierce is not, however, a solo adventure. The lioness does not sit alone; the Beyhive is always close by; the march is filled with thousands. Each *Fierce* individual we know does not do it despite others, on the backs of others, or to hurt others. This is why we are so attracted to fierce people. It's why we want to know them, be around them, and be like them. In fact, what attracts us most to the fierceness is the level of open-minded adventure that appears at the surface as freedom.

You might imagine someone who jumps out of airplanes or quits their job to go travel the world as fierce and while those people certainly are not risk-averse, it is not the kind of adventure I am referring to. *Fierce* individuals draw you in because they want to know you, hear your opinions, be open to a good debate, and be willing to make the decisions about the new restaurant to try, the next vacation destination, or the mountain to hike. Truly *Fierce* individuals want to enjoy the journey with others, they understand the value of human connection, and they want to bring others along for the ride.

Let's talk about the *Fierce* individual for a moment as it's important to identify their uniqueness. *Fierce* individuals speak their mind, stand up for a cause and even against authority when authority is wrong, and do the right thing because it is the right thing to do. You will find these individuals fighting against injustice and taking on helping those who cannot defend themselves. The passion for life is what generates their desire to speak up for those who do not have the same opportunities or the courage to speak on their own. *Fierce* individuals know vulnerability and courage. They are brave because at some point in their life they were witnessed to or experienced themselves, shame, prejudice, inequality, abuse, and the wounded spirits of generations that came before us. They "speak truth to bullshit" as Brené Brown would say and want to nurture our humanity.

So, what is it that you whisper to yourself? What do you believe to be true about you? Are you *Fierce*? Do you want to be? I believe we all have it within ourselves when equipped with the right tools in our tool belt to be *Fierce* and embrace the power of owning your journey. I was inspired to write this book because I have coached and mentored so many people over the years, through many phases of life, that want to move forward in their career, their business, or their personal relationships. But they either feel stuck or like they are on that hamster wheel living the same day over and over.

In this book you will find a six-step guide for getting off that wheel, getting unstuck, and moving ahead with your goals. If you want that next promotion in your career, I can help you. If you want to leave your 9-5 and start your own business, I can help you. If you want to accomplish your personal goals, I can help you. It is time to stop putting the "shoulda woulda coulda's" on the shelf and dust them off.

Now is the time to embrace the *Fierce* within you; stop saying yes to everyone else and start saying yes to you! There could not be a better time for you to be holding this book in your hands. With all the changes that 2020 has brought to our lives, now is the best time to develop the next step for your career, business, or personal journey. While the thought of developing a strategy might seem overwhelming, I applaud you for investing in this book because if one thing is for sure…the fastest path to success is to learn from other successful people.

I know firsthand the power of getting clear and intentional on your values, coordinating your life in an organized way, having a communication plan to externally put yourself out there, collaborating and building a network, using creative tools to see your future, and

4

understanding your competitive advantage. As a leader, mother, and doctorate student, I know with certainty that when you study and apply what I am teaching in this book you will succeed in taking your journey to the next level!

My approach has contributed not only to my own success but to the friends, colleagues, and entrepreneurs who have worked with me. I can talk the talk and walk the walk! The best thing you can do for yourself is to take this book and use it as a simple step-by-step guide. The accompanying tools and tips throughout the book as well as the available coaching program are wonderful gifts for you. Study the book, do the work, and put the ideas into practice in your life, and you will be sure to reach your goals. May you *Fiercely* own your journey and embrace the power of each step along the way!

Fierce is to be intimately aware of one's purpose, values, strengths, and dreams such that the journey is filled with an intense passion for life.

Clarity of Values

Without a doubt 2020 has surely been relentless, the impacts have been felt on our health, our jobs, our families, and quite honestly our dreams. Do you remember back in January thinking you were overwhelmed by personal and professional responsibilities? Did you ever think you would add new responsibilities and skills like teaching your children how to navigate distance learning or managing relationships with colleagues and friends over Zoom? Every time you got the hang of it something new managed to pile on. Thankfully I had

Glennon Doyle's *Untamed* to remind me "We can do hard things" (if you haven't read it yet I highly recommend it!).

If I had asked you to make a list of your priorities last year and you compared that to now, you may be surprised to see how many things were so important to you a year ago and are simply irrelevant today. It is important to remember that all the tools I am going to share with you throughout this book are living techniques meaning it's not something you do once, check off your list, and move onto the next how-to guide. They are the six C's of your strategy and like all good plans they will need reflecting, updating, and the flexibility to pivot when life changes.

The first step in building your new strategy is to get explicitly clear on your values. If you are wondering how values have anything to do with strategy, let me tell you, it is the most critical step. A value is something you find to be very important and it may be a belief, a behavior, or a principle that you deem worthy. Values are different from priorities or responsibilities - they have a gravity that roots you in purpose. Sometimes it can be very easy to identify your values, however, if I asked you (which I will) to write them down, prioritize them, and then shape every activity you do around them, you might start to question what you believe to be your core values.

Glennon Doyle provides a great example of finding this clarity, "if you sit with what pisses you off and breaks your heart, that will be a big red arrow pointing you towards your purpose." Another way to look at this can be the things that drive you, the fire in your belly, the passions you can't imagine life without, the reason you wake up each day. Remember these are YOUR values. Not the values of your family, your friends, or others around you.

You may have values similar to your inner circle and your community. In fact, many of those external factors shape our values however make sure to spend some time in this chapter and on the upcoming exercises, as knowing your values will shape the rest of the strategy you develop. One of my favorite authors, professor, and *Fierce* woman, who I will quote and refer to throughout this book, is Brené Brown. Her adaptation of Theodore Roosevelt's 'Man in the Arena' speech inspired me during her infamous *Why Your Critics Aren't The Ones That Count* talk at the 2013 99U's creatives conference. She stated, "if you aren't in the arena also getting your ass kicked then I'm not interested in your feedback." So, what does it mean to be in the arena?

Being truly vulnerable and possessing courage to allow you to step into the arena is one thing, but the way you survive is having your values tattooed on your skin for everyone to see – even the critics. In her book *Dare to Lead*, Brené states "integrity is choosing courage over comfort; it's choosing what's right over what's fun, fast, or easy; and it's practicing your values, not just professing them." For me integrity is a core value, it shows up in everything I do, every action I take, and everything I aspire to do. Knowing it is one of my values, I can design my strategy around this core principle. Finding your values is the first place we will start, but keep in mind it is not what you tell others you believe – it is what you whisper to yourself.

In **Values Exercise 1 - Part 1** (p. 18-20) you will find a list of values. These are only examples so please feel free to add in your own. I have provided you with 175 values and I want you to take out a notebook and write down every one of the words that you identify with. It is important to actually write them down so avoid circling them in the book or typing them out on a computer. The act of writing commits to your brain in a different way and you will need the list you form to move on to part two in this exercise. Here is the secret recipe – do not just write down words that sound good, remember what I described above about values that root you in purpose, choose words that inspire, motivate, and feel authentic to you. Do not overthink it and if it resonates with you then write it down. There is no magic number of values here so it's okay to have a long list or a short list.

In **Values Exercise 1 - Part 2** (p. 21) you will now put the list of values you created into collections or groups. The key here is to have no more than five groupings so I suggest making five squares or "buckets" in your notebook. As you think about each value on your list, start collecting similar values together in each bucket. You may find as you go through this exercise that some of the values just don't fit into similar groups and you may end up dropping them from the list. It's very important not to create a sixth or seventh bucket (if you are the type of person who does not like being limited to five this exercise is especially for you – believe me!). I know it will be hard to narrow your list into five collections so if you find yourself frustrated then take a break, sleep on it, and come back to the list when you are ready. You can do this and trust me it is going to be worth it - I promise!

Let me tell you about an entrepreneur I work with. She has amazing ideas, a true connection to purpose on this earth, and is just generally a genuine person you want to be around. She has invested countless hours, dollars, and relationships in building each one of her businesses. For the sake of this story let's call her Abigail. I received a call one day from Abigail asking how I balance everything I have on my plate? I asked her if she was feeling overwhelmed and to my surprise, she was actually feeling very motivated.

Abigail, you see, was managing eight different ventures (yes - I said 8), and she knew she was at a place where she was ready to close out two of them. Where she was stuck however was making the decision between investing more time and money in self-growth and development seminars (which she loves, values, and knows they help her to improve) and getting what she believed to be her most important business off the ground. I knew this was going to be more than just a phone call, so I offered to spend a day with her.

Abigail and I spent an entire Saturday going through everything she had on her plate at that very moment and it became very clear to me in the first hour that I needed to help her with clarity of values. I was confident she knew what was important to her, but I believed she was struggling to prioritize which meant she was saying "Yes" to everything that came her way. Sometimes we do this for a fear of missing out, a belief that each opportunity could get us some great reward, or out of obligation to existing relationships or networks we have, and we just don't want to say no to anyone.

In Abigail's case, it was the second choice. She did not want to miss out on opportunities that she believed could help grow her businesses, bring in income, or personally make her better. What I saw in her that day however was an over-extended (physically, emotionally, and financially) entrepreneur with amazing potential who simply needed to get explicit with her values. Abigail was using every tool most of us think of when trying to get organized. She had a large whiteboard, butcher paper with sticky notes all over it, a planner notebook where she organized her time, a computer program for organizing her notes, and file folders filled with (I mean FILLED) scratch paper full of lists, ideas, and notes she had taken from workshops.

Abigail was using every tool she thought possible to help her with balancing these eight businesses that she was either owner of, co-owner, or consultant for. As I sat on the floor of her office, file folders with a label maker in front of me, I told her let's pause for a moment. I took out my notebook and started to ask her questions. I could immediately tell she was thinking "why are you interviewing me, we have so much work to do, just tell me what to do!" I knew that giving her the answer I thought best may not in fact be the right answer for her. I have different values than she does.

Another great book released this year *Think Like a Monk* by Jay Shetty talks about values as well. Jay states "I felt the urge to be around people who had the values I wanted not the things I wanted." This was true of my relationship with Abigail, we had similar values and it's why she trusted me to help her. However, similar values do not equal the same values. If I was going to help her, I needed Abigail to make the decisions best for her that aligned with her own values.

So, I asked her to tell me all the things she was working on. I wanted to know why each of them meant something to her, why they were hard to let go of or why they were stuck, and what she envisioned each of them to be. While she talked, I wrote, I captured words and themes that started to appear. Without her realizing what I was doing, I took Abigail through Exercise 1. Then I let her know the four areas that appeared to collect together.

Now for **Values Exercise 1 - Part 3** (p. 22) you will review the collections or buckets of values you have come up with. In each of the five areas you have chosen, I want you to circle the one word that best represents that collection of values. Try to not overthink this and pick the word that resonates with you. Remember integrity is choosing courage over comfort so do not be afraid to select the word in each bucket that you feel intimidated by or that provokes something within you – those feelings are there for a reason. Don't forget what Glennon said about it pissing you off or breaking your heart, as there is a grounding that happens in each of us when we see a value that is our own. Did you commit? Do you have your 5 Core Values? How do you feel?

Remember developing a strategy is a process and it is not meant to be done overnight, rushed, or cheated. You want to feel good about this first step, and I know it is so incredibly hard to pare down 175 values to just 5, but you did it. So now you sit with these five values. Marinate on how they make you feel. Having clarity of values is not easy work and it is why many companies and successful people struggle with developing their mission and vision statements.

Earlier this year in an interview with Simon Sinek, the infamous *Start With Why* author, he said "the goal is not to do business with everybody who needs what you have, the goal is to do business with people who believe what you believe." He elaborates that having shared values allows trust to form more deeply and in developing company culture we all know how important trust is. The same can be said about you. If you are not clear on what you value, then how can an employer trust you and give you that promotion? How can a customer hire you or purchase your product? How can you take that next step to accomplish your goals?

This is the part in the book where we celebrate! You have selected five core values that are exactly right for where you are today. I want you to add these to your whiteboards, vision boards, place them on sticky notes above your bed - get creative it's not about the how. It's about what you have selected. I also want you to take a deep breath in and a long slow exhale out (yes I am telling you to breathe) and as you

14

exhale I want you to feel the values you have selected like a warm blanket enveloping you.

This is who you are, this is what you believe, these are the things most sacred and important to you.

And here is the important thing to remember - just as you grow and change, so do your values. So many of us are hard-wired to believe that our values were learned or accepted in the way we were raised and that we must fight to hold onto those, protect them, and in some very extreme cases die for them. My advice to you and to anyone is that you would never put a tree in a small pot – why, because as it grows its roots need space to expand. The roots that began out of the seedling will be with it, but so will new roots that form as it grows. Do not limit yourself or your way of thinking. Values grow and change along with us throughout this amazing journey we are on.

Can you think of a person or a company who closed off their roots by keeping them in a small pot? Most of us are aware of the Blockbuster or Kodak examples, right? I am sure those company CEO's led their teams through a similar exercise to define their values, develop their mission and vision, and then they slapped them on a poster, a PowerPoint, or a bulletin board and that is where they later died. So how can you ensure that the values you have selected today do not keep other new values from forming? You must carve out time to repeat this exercise. That is why I suggested the notebook and not simply writing in the pages of this book.

This is a living tool that can help you throughout your career, your business, or your life. How often should you complete it? My advice is, at minimum, to do it once per year. I will suggest that if you are going to start something big and new in your life like a new job, a new business, or a new relationship that you repeat it. These interchanges in life present the best opportunity for reflection and each time you do this you will find it's not as hard as the first time you sat with all 175 words.

I realize there is a large contingency of those reading this book that are ready to move onto the next section because they are so motivated by the first tool. And then there is a smaller portion of you who are so mentally exhausted that you are halfway contemplating putting the book down and calling it quits. I see you; I know you; I am you. Most days I am the first group, tackling the to-do list, the instructions, and checking every box off until it's done. On some days, however, I am in the second group - tired of trying to improve, exhausted from every personal growth and development exercise (believe me I have tried them all), and ready to accept that I am the way I am.

What I know to be true is that being *Fierce* does not mean you are at 100% all the time. It does not mean you won't rumble with yourself and tap out. Being Fierce does mean however that you get back up tomorrow and get right back at it because you know you are worthy and passionate about life.

You have tackled the first C in the six-step plan – **Clarity of Values**. Let me ask you now, before we move ahead with the next step, how do those values measure up with what is ahead of you? Do they align with the company you work for and the promotion or position you want to go after? Do they resonate with the business you are developing or are running, and if so, are you doing business with people whose values are aligned to yours? How about in your personal life? Are the people you surround yourself with aware of what you value? These are questions you want to think about as we head into the next section. If any of the parts in **Values Exercise 1** brought about questions, anxieties, or confusion this is where my available consulting may be the right answer for you. I am available for a free thirty-minute call to review any of your needs and evaluate how I can help. Simply email yourfiercestrategy@gmail.com and know you are not alone in this process.

Values Exercise 1 – Part 1

Abundance	Expressiveness	Personal Development
Acceptance	Facilitation	Playfulness
Accountability	Fairness	Popularity
Achievement	Faith	Power
Advancement	Fame	Preparedness
Adventure	Family	Pride in Your Work
Advocacy	Finances	Proactivity
Affection	Finesse	Professionalism
Ambition	Fitness	Prosperity
Appreciation	Flexibility	Punctuality
Attractiveness	Forgiveness	Quality
Autonomy	Freedom	Reciprocity
Balance	Friendship	Recognition
Be True	Fun	Relationships
Beauty	Fun-Loving	Reliability
Being the Best	Generosity	Religion
Benevolence	Giving People a Chance	Renewal
Boldness	Goodness	Resilience
Brilliance	Grace	Resourcefulness
Calmness	Gratitude	Respect
Career	Growth	Responsibility

Caring	Happiness	Responsiveness
Challenge	Harmony	Risk Taking
Change	Health	Safety
Charisma	Home	Security
Charity	Honesty	Self-Control
Cheerfulness	Humanity	Selflessness
Clarity	Humility	Self-Respect
Cleverness	Humor	Service
Collaboration	Inclusiveness	Simplicity
Commitment	Independence	Speed
Commonality	Individuality	Spirituality
Communication	Innovation	Stability
Community	Inspiration	Strength
Compassion	Integrity	Success
Connection	Intelligence	Teamwork
Consistency	Intuition	Thankfulness
Contentment	Invention	This Too Shall Pass Attitude
Contribution	Involvement	Thoughtfulness
Cooperation	Joy	Traditionalism
Courage	Justice	Trusting Your Gut
Creativity	Kindness	Trustworthiness
Credibility	Knowledge	Understanding
Curiosity	Leadership	Uniqueness

Daring	Learning	Usefulness
Decisiveness	Love	Versatility
Dedication	Love of Career	Vision
Dependability	Loyalty	Warmth
Diversity	Making a Difference	Wealth
Effectiveness	Mindfulness	Well-Being
Empathy	Motivation	Wellness
Encouragement	Open-Mindedness	Willingness
Endurance	Optimism	Wisdom
Enjoyment	Order	Work Smarter and Harder
Entertain	Originality	Zeal
Enthusiasm	Passion	Add your own
Entrepreneurial	Patience	
Ethics	Peace	
Excellence	Perfection	
Excitement	Performance	

Values Exercise 1 – Part 2

Accountability Credibility Honesty Integrity Trustworthiness
Respect Self-Respect Leadership Strength Resilience
Compassion Understanding Empathy Humanity Making a Difference
Open-Mindedness Diversity Inclusiveness Fairness
Family Friends Love Passion

Values Exercise 1 – Part 3

Accountability
Credibility
Honesty
(Integrity)
Trustworthiness

Respect
Self-Respect
Leadership
Strength
(Resilience)

Compassion
Understanding
Empathy
Humanity
(Making a Difference)

Diversity
Inclusiveness
(Open-Mindedness)
Fairness

(Family)
Friends
Love
Passion

Coordination

"You either walk inside your story and own it or you stand outside your story and hustle for your worthiness."

— Brené Brown

You made it! Those freshly tattooed values may still be healing, but you are ready to do something with them, right? Were you surprised to see the Brené quote at the start of this section? (I warned you) There is something so empowering about standing firm in your values, your convictions, the roots to your tree. Those five core values you chose are now going to help you shape the next step in your strategy. This is where all the Marie Kondo fans, or the Lean & Six Sigma geeks get really excited.

It's time to get organized and not sock drawer organized, but tangible daily life responsibilities and tasks organized. Maybe this means the sock drawer for you if you are a start-up sock entrepreneur, but for most of you reading this book it means the second C in your *Fierce* strategy – Coordination.

Each plan you make in life, as motivating as it might be, has the potential to be placed on a shelf somewhere, left to collect dust bunnies, and admired when it becomes trash on a spring-cleaning kind of day. You did not buy this book because you wanted a pretty teal covered manuscript on your shelf. You bought it because something about *Fierce* called out to you and said, "now is your time" and "I can do six steps, that's easy." Developing a strategy is simply the energy you have decided to put into something you deem important. And now that you have decided having a strategy is important to you, let's ensure you can sustain it.

The tools in this section are also active things you will do each day and before long they will become muscle memory and second nature to you. Simon Sinek said "vision is a destination, a fixed point to which we focus all effort. Strategy is a route, an adaptable path to get us where we want to go." Let's start to formulate the tactics and tools you need to manage and adapt the strategy you are developing.

Recall at the start of this book, you can use each of these tools regardless of your desired outcome. If you are trying to make a career move, level up your business, or make a change in your personal life, learning how to organize your time and energy is very important.

Abigail who you met in the last section was the perfect client for what I am about to teach you next. Once she could clearly see the four areas she valued, she then asked me "what do I do first?" This is where the $100 exercise became her challenge.

I shared with Abigail that if I was going to invest in her (imagine I am some Silicon Valley Venture Capitalist) and she was going to pitch me her values, how much of my $100 should I invest in each of her four areas? Another way to think of this is how would you spend your $100 if you were investing in the stock market? Would you buy $1 share in 100 companies or would you select a smaller number of companies so you could have more stock in each of them?

In **Coordination Exercise 2 – Part 1** (p. 34) I want you to list your 5 core values on a new page in your notebook. Next to each value, I want you to invest part of your $100. There are no right or wrong answers here. You can place $20 in each of them or you can place $50 in one of them and divide the rest accordingly. I encourage you however to try hard not to assign the same exact amount of money to more than one category. If you do decide they are all worth $20 each then I am going to challenge you to go back and rank them.

In Abigail's case, she assigned her four values as $40, $25, $20, $15. Reflect back to when you were choosing the one word in each of the value buckets that resonated with you or that summarized that collection the best. By pairing down the list to just five you got this amazing sense of clarity, right? The same is happening here. All 5 of your core values are important, that is why you chose them however you have a natural order within them that starts to surface as you assign monetary value to them.

Let me share with you a story as I have had to put this into practice in my corporate job. In any business, you have limited capital resources (this is the money available to reinvest in yourself) and sometimes you must make hard choices about who gets money for investment now versus later. The $100 exercise was something I learned at a strategy retreat a few years back as we had generated ideas for capital investment in our company. Our VP at the time then said to us, "well if you only have $100 which things do you choose?" I remember the air in the room just deflated not because of what she was asking us, but because the reality of money, time, and resources were so limiting.

The same reality can be applied to your life and your values. You do not have an endless amount of time or energy, so while the five values are all so very important, they cannot all be working forces at the same exact time. Now that you have assigned parts of your $100 to each of your five core values, I want you to turn the page in your notebook (don't worry we will come back to them).

In **Coordination Exercise 2 – Part 2** (p. 35) I want you to list all your responsibilities. To help you organize these thoughts I suggest making three columns on your page; daily, weekly, and monthly responsibilities, as most everything you do will fall into these columns. This is a snapshot in time as I am fully aware responsibilities change as life changes. For now, just go with me and list out everything. Many of you reading this wear many hats in life so the thought of listing out your responsibilities may seem daunting.

You have your work responsibilities, your home responsibilities, your parenting or relationship responsibilities (yes there are tasks to be done in relationships), and your community or citizenship responsibilities. While you may be tempted to make separate responsibilities lists, I challenge you to fit them within the three columns - daily, weekly, monthly. Remember there are only 24 hours a day and the list are not for what you wish were your responsibilities, it is for what is tangibly your day-in and day-out duties.

Making a list of your responsibilities is not something you should overthink either. It is not meant to make you feel overwhelmed, guilty, or any negative emotion whatsoever. The list is simply part of a tool I am going to help you with so that the hamster wheel we talked about can feel like a walk along the beach instead. In order to help you get there, I need you to be able to see what you are doing, how often, and for whom. This list you are making may not be exhaustive and I am sure you could add things to it if you did this over a few days, but do not worry if it's not perfect. The important part is to see the types of things you are responsible for.

In **Coordination Exercise 2 – Part 3** (p. 36) you will go through each of your daily, weekly, and monthly responsibilities and circle the ones that align to your five core values. You will have things that align on the list and things that do not align – this is part of the process. What you are doing now is clearly identifying which of your responsibilities are "value" and which are "non-value." There are many responsibilities in our life that are "non-value" yet are necessary to maintain life, I refer to these fondly as necessary evils. For instance, you may have listed personal hygiene on your daily tasks – this does not necessarily align to your values however it is a necessary evil to avoid poor health. At the end of this part, you should be able to see your "value" and "non-value" responsibilities.

I vividly remember the first time I completed this exercise in my career. I was a front-line supervisor at the time, responsible for multiple operational clinics spread across multiple locations. I recall being asked to complete my list during an all-day workshop we were participating in as lean leaders. The purpose of this particular task was to help us as leaders to develop our leader's standard work and I have modified it over the years because it is applicable to all aspects of life. One of the senior leaders in the organization at the time shared his definition of value as "developing your people, developing yourself, developing your team, and developing your organization."

These four key areas helped us to see if the tasks we were doing as leaders each day, week, or month were value-add and aligned with this definition or non-value add. We each set goals to limit the percentage of non-value tasks in our leader's standard work so we truly could have a culture of developing people. As lean leaders in the organization, we wanted to remove the non-value and wasteful items with the support of our one up's who were there to remove barriers. Trying to remove items off the list was extremely hard and yet we noticed new things were being consistently added. The coaching we received at the time was, "first you must see what is a value add and non-value add, second you must be able to identify what is getting in the way or preventing you from more value add tasks, and finally, it was okay to escalate when these barriers arose."

In life, however, who can you escalate to if the tasks on your lists do not align to your values and are not those "necessary evils" for maintaining life? This is where the power of saying yes to you comes into play. It is ok to say "in order to complete responsibility A which aligns to my core values, I must remove or decrease the frequency of responsibility B." How often do you hear someone say, "I don't have the time" or the wise old saying "you permit what you promote?" If it is important to you then you will find the time, or you will buy this book so I can help you find the time!

You still have that values page in your notebook with the assigned $100? Now is the time where we crosswalk your core values assessment with your responsibilities list. Every dollar you assigned to the five core values is the percentage of the time you should be devoting to it. Let me elaborate with Abigail's story as an example. When she knew that she would invest $40 of her $100 in the business she was trying to get up and going, I asked her to convert 40% of her time to the responsibilities necessary to live out this value. The same went for the $25 she wanted to invest in self-growth and development, I asked her to spend 25% of her time on those specific tasks.

This is where I spent almost two hours with Abigail talking out scenario after scenario that she was facing in the next two weeks where she would have to make choices that aligned with these new allocations of time. One example she provided was choosing between attending a three-day workshop she was interested in versus finishing up a few projects that would bring her new income. We went back and forth as I listened to her describe how she needed more funds to invest in her new business however she really wanted to learn some of the skills at the workshop. In the end, Abigail realized that the workshop would be offered again later, and the immediate priority was finishing the income-generating projects.

The final **Coordination Exercise 2 – Part 4** (p. 37) is setting up your schedule and time in order to be doing the valuable work that you have decided is important to you. On a new page in your notebook start with the first core value that you assigned the most percentage of time. Then underneath it, list all the responsibilities associated with it. Do this with each of the five core values until you have a separate set of responsibilities each associated with your core values. Then take all of those responsibilities that were "non-value" and start to decide which ones are still necessary evils and which ones do not serve either purpose. Today is the day you commit to removing those responsibilities or doing them infrequently until you can plan to remove them.

I want you to spend time doing what makes you Fierce.

Once you have your values and aligned responsibilities list you will have completed the hardest steps in strategy development. Time to celebrate once more – you did it! Two incredibly thoughtful, time-consuming tasks are now complete and are the backbone of everything we will do together throughout the rest of this book. I have provided a few examples at the end of the exercises so you can have a visual sense of what this all looks like when it's completed. For all of you who love excel spreadsheets – this is a great time to transfer what you wrote in the notebook into an organized platform so be sure to check out that example. If you prefer a less analytical tool you can also do this on a visual whiteboard. We will be talking a lot more about that in the sections to come so feel free to just let them live in your notebook for now.

If any of the parts in **Exercise 2** brought about questions, anxieties, or confusion this is where my available consulting may be the right answer for you. I am available for a free thirty-minute call to review any of your needs and evaluate how I can help. Simply email yourfiercestrategy@gmail.com and know you are not alone in this process. Time to take another deep breath in and exhale out. Close your eyes, you can now step off the hamster wheel, feel the sand beneath your toes, the sound of the ocean near you, and the breeze against your face. Let's start walking along the beach.

Coordination Exercise 2 – Part 1

Core Value	$100 Exercise
Integrity	$30
Resilience	$10
Making a Difference	$15
Open-Mindedness	$10
Family	$35

Coordination Exercise 2 – Part 2

Responsibilities

Daily	Weekly	Monthly
Prepare Meals for Family	Grocery Shop	Costco Trip
Take kids to and from school, check homework, ensure reading is complete	Take kids to activities	Help with school projects
Work (8-10 hours)	Sync work calendar and home calendar	Attend Work Sponsored Events
Hygiene Routine	Exercise	Massage
Laundry	Household cleaning	Outdoor cleaning
Reading for School	Papers for School	Student Ambassador duties
Check Email/Social Media sites/Texts	Networking Activities	Volunteer Activities
Watch Television	Watch a Movie	Binge a Netflix Show
Sleep	Nap	Stay in PJ's for a whole Saturday
Journal	Connect with Friends and Family	Consider Dating

Coordination Exercise 2 – Part 3

Responsibilities

Daily	Weekly	Monthly
Prepare Meals for Family	Grocery Shop	Costco Trip
Take kids to and from school, check homework, ensure reading is complete	Take kids to activities	Help with school projects
Work (8-10 hours)	Sync work calendar and home calendar	Attend Work Sponsored Events
Hygiene Routine	Exercise	Massage
Laundry	Household cleaning	Outdoor cleaning
Reading for School	Papers for School	Student Ambassador duties
Check Email/Social Media sites/Texts	Networking Activities	Volunteer Activities
Watch Television	Watch a Movie	Binge a Netflix Show
Sleep	Nap	Stay in PJ's for a whole Saturday
Journal	Connect with Friends and Family	Consider Dating

Coordination Exercise 2 – Part 4

Core Value	% of Time
Integrity Work & School	30%
Resilience Exercise, Massage, Journal, Sleep?	10%
Making a Difference Volunteer Activities, Work Events, Student Ambassador Duties	15%
Open-Mindedness Networking Activities, Dating?	10%
Family Caring for kids and their school/activities & Connecting with Family and Friends	35%
Non-Value Household chores, food prep, shopping, TV, Social Media, Some of the Events	0%

Communication

"Communication works best when we combine appropriateness with authenticity, finding that sweet spot where opinions are not brutally honest but delicately honest."

— Sheryl Sandberg

There are thousands of books on communication so do not worry - this is not adding one more to the pile. Communication is, however, a large part of strategic development. In the first two steps, clarity of values and coordination, you worked internally to identify, prioritize, and organize your values and responsibilities. This was the work to find your authenticity. Believe it or not, you can no longer show up with the beliefs, behaviors, and principles of others because you are now explicitly clear about your own values.

Now it is time to start communicating those outwardly as it will help you to minimize the obligations you feel saying yes to others over saying yes to you. When people around you can see, feel, and know the values you have prioritized, an amazing thing will start to happen, they will want to be around and admire the *Fierce* individual they interact with. Glennon Doyle said "brave means living from the inside out. Brave means, in every uncertain moment, turning inward, feeling for the Knowing, and speaking it out loud." Having the courage and vulnerability to be *Fierce* has already started to happen for you.

Choosing your core values and aligning your life's responsibilities accordingly is brave. Now I want to show you how to strengthen those choices and set your external part of the strategy. This is going to require intention. If you have made it this far into the book, then I know you are committed to finishing your plan but being intentional in how you communicate is going to take even more commitment.

Experiencing corporate strategy for most people happens the moment a company deploys its communication plan. After countless hours in business development teams, approvals from layers of leadership, and final sign off by a Board of Directors, the organizations strategy gets communicated out to all of its employees and then eventually it's clients and customers. Communication can come in the form of emails, printed posters, social media campaigns, and for most companies a public Annual Report.

For the companies that are really good at communicating their values and strategy, you can see clear line of sight by asking the most front line of employees – what is your company's strategy? If they can answer the question, then you know the organization has done a great job communicating it. Unfortunately, what you will find across most industries, is that when you ask five different employees what the company strategy is you will get five different answers. This is because communicating the strategy can get lost in translation if it is not simple and explicitly clear.

The four sections I am going to share with you regarding your communication strategy include **calendaring (time-blocking), resumes, interviews, social media and marketing**. Each of these areas may seem like basic tasks that you feel you have already accomplished or have a routine for. Let me, however, ask you - how are they working for you? Some of you reading this may feel like there is never enough time to accomplish what you set out to do. Some may feel like you can't find the dream job you want or get past the application and get an interview. How about those of you who are starting businesses or trying to improve your business and struggled with social media and marketing. There are sections that may resonate with only some of you however I encourage you to check out each one because they will all link to the first two parts of the plan you have already developed. This is all a part of the *Fierce* journey.

Simon Sinek shared "we are drawn to leaders and organizations that are good at communicating what they believe. Their ability to make us feel like we belong, to make us feel special, safe, and not alone is part of what gives them the ability to inspire us." To illustrate this, let me tell you a tale of two Carolines. The first is a woman whom I hired many years ago and then helped her get to the next level in her career. The second is a woman I met at a professional conference a few years back who was struggling to balance multiple personal and professional responsibilities.

Caroline and Carolyne are both perfect examples of how external communication strategies can open the door for your career, business, and life. What I admire in both are their genuine and transparent values which is why these *Fierce* women just needed some help crafting their message.

Caroline was at a place in her career where she was feeling the strain of the 'glass ceiling' as the decades of experience she had in both education and quality were limited by the fact that she worked for an organization that would not advance her past a front line manager role. This was in large part due to the fact that the organization had a faith-based strategy and while she was of faith, it was not their denomination. When she finally was brave enough to confront her director on the issue of professional growth and development, she got the honest answer she dreaded. At the time we had a mutual friend who knew that I was hiring for a leadership position and that Caroline was ready to leave her organization. We will address the power of a network in the next section, but keep in mind that half the battle of getting the interview is having someone on the inside you know of or who knows you.

After an initial call with Caroline, I knew she was "my kind of people" meaning she worked her butt off and just needed someone to give her a chance. I had been in that place previously in my career and committed to returning the favor that had once been given to me. It's not a promise of a job, however, it is the commitment to at least give the person an interview. It is then their role to earn the job. After I brought her in to interview with my team, she and I both realized she was overqualified.

She had all the knowledge and expertise, but what lacked was the titles on her resume for a human resource recruiter to give her a management position she deserved as well as the salary range, she was worth. Caroline had two options in front of her - stay in the role, where she was at a comfortable salary, knowing she would never advance, or take the leadership role with me and earn the necessary operational experience needed to propel her to the next level. I am sure you can guess what she decided.

Over the next year, I coached and mentored her until a senior management role became available. Developing her resume to highlight her accomplishments in each role and adequately portraying the experience she had was our first step. Then came practicing interview questions with her so each panel she would experience would get to know the authentic her. One of her areas of opportunity was in her stoic responses, which for Caroline meant a calm appearance. However, to the interview panel she appeared aloof.

Caroline also could not hide her emotion and she became flushed with any reaction the interview brought out in her. We practiced frequently; this was the best way to get her prepared for anything they might ask. The most important thing is she had a plan – a strategy – and Caroline garnered the well-deserved position.

Carolyne appeared, at the onset of meeting her, to have it all together. The kind of woman who I thought could actually mentor me. Our meeting was no coincidence as I realized we were both meant to help one another. The conference we attended was for women in leadership and had many breakout sessions that gave tips and tricks for all the usual self-growth and development stuff. I remember sitting next to her in one particular session and in my mind, I was thinking "I could teach this session – and do it better" - not from an arrogant place, but rather, I realized the presenter was not connecting with the audience. Carolyne must have been feeling disconnected as well because she leaned over to me and said, "there is no there - there." We started talking quietly to ourselves and decided to step out and grab a coffee.

Carolyne was a successful leader, mother, wife, and community advocate. She tried to balance her professional responsibilities at work, her personal responsibilities at home, and her desire to give back to her community as a member of three non-profit organizations. As you can see, we hit it off because Carolyne was also "my kind of people." The beautiful thing about her was the service heart she had and yet it was the very thing that was stressing her out. She did not know how to say no to anyone. People knew they could rely on her and as such her calendar was overcommitted to say the least.

I asked her what she wanted to get out of the conference we were attending to which she replied, "better time management tools or techniques." She felt like there was not enough time in the day, week, month to get all of the thigs done that were so important to her. She felt like she was failing everyone around her and only giving 30 percent to each commitment instead of 100 percent. Sound familiar?

John Rohn, American Entrepreneur, author, and motivational speaker once said, "Effective communication is 20% what you know and 80% how you feel about what you know." The first place we must start when coordinating our lives is to set the intention. You can no longer feel like these changes are important or wish you had the tools in your tool belt - you must decide to take the steps to organize your life - so they align to your values. In **Coordination E2/P4** you created a list of your five core values and the associated percentage of time you need to spend on each of them. This is where we take the 'what' you learned, and I show you 'how' to apply it. Time-blocking is a common technique that helps brings your life into focus.

Calendaring (Time-Blocking)

How many times have you started out with a to-do list for the day or week and then only accomplished 1-2 of those things? How often do you have moments of distraction that take you away from the important tasks you wanted to get done? Well, time-blocking may not solve every possible distraction, but it is a technique that I live by. I developed the early parts of my technique the first time I bought a planner. From a very young age I was planning my life, and this is how intentionality first showed up for me. Most people know how to use their calendar (whether computer, smartphone app, or good ol' fashioned notebook kind) in order to block off time for health appointments, special holidays/birthdays/anniversaries they want to remember, and other tasks like travel plans.

I use my calendar to block off almost every task in my life. First because being able to visually see what I am doing, when I am doing it, and with whom, is a helpful technique for staying on track for my goals. Secondly, I also enjoy looking back and reflecting on how I felt when the week or month was over, giving myself affirmation for all that was accomplished, and then setting the next plan forward. Each of us has the thing in our life that is so important to us that we keep close track of it.

For my father, he kept track of every penny he spent. Pen and small paper in his pocket at all times so even the smallest $1.25 didn't go untraced. These were before the days of fancy spreadsheets and apps to track your spending. This technique of tracking expenses rubbed off on me and I remember being the only girl in my college dorm putting my expenses into an Excel spreadsheet.

I also know many colleagues who take detailed notes every day, all day, and have countless notebooks full of things they want to be able to reference and remember. For others, keeping track of photos, mementos, and sentimental items is like a religion. The point here is that if it is important to you, then you will take the time to develop the new skill, habit, or technique. I can promise you that time-blocking is essential to taking control of your life and accomplishing your goals. Keeping track of your time also does not have to be overly complicated. I remember the first time that I ran into a frustrating conflict at work where a reoccurring meeting was scheduled during a time that I had carved out for project work. Well, at least I thought I had carved it out. Turns out that I had never 'blocked' that time off on my calendar, so the slot was then taken by this new meeting. If you don't decide what is a priority in your calendar, I guarantee others will decide it for you!

In **Communication Exercise 3 – Part 1** (p. 69) I want you to start time-blocking one week of your life. For the sake of the exercise, you can use an Outlook calendar, smartphone app, or a paper notebook calendar – whichever is your normal go to type. Make sure it's a blank week and be sure to follow the example I provide you. The first important step is to carve out the routine stuff or the 'necessary evils' as I referred to in the last section. Maybe this means from 6-8 a.m. every day you have the morning routine carved out in order to get yourself and others ready, fed, and motivated for the day. This can include your exercise routine if this is something important to you as well. While we all take for granted this usual routine practice every morning, all it takes is one day when you are asked to be somewhere early to throw off the entire day. Carve out the time and block it from being scheduled by something else.

Then your next task should be the allotted time needed each day to get jump-started on your work, business, or daily commitment. For many people, this looks like checking emails, following up on tasks, and scheduling new commitments. Notice I did not say wake up and check email! I am sure with all of our smart phones we are guilty of looking at emails, social media accounts, and bank accounts before our eyes are ever fully awake, but this is a bad habit to try and break. Give yourself time in the morning to truly rise and not be distracted by all the things on that phone. Nothing is ever an emergency, and if it were, they would have called, right?

So, back to time-blocking your email - can you commit to three times a day instead of being glued to it all day long? Many studies are showing how much more productive you can be if you set aside dedicated time to do email instead of attending to it all throughout the day. The next necessary tasks are to add in any appointments for your personal health, wellness, and those for your family that you must commit to. Make sure these are always a top priority. Finally add in your lunch and evening routine. A lesson learned from my boss – if you don't carve out time for lunch, you won't eat, and no one will be checking to make sure you are fed. Now you should be able to see a week of your life with just the basic necessities in it.

Sometime in the morning, sometime in the afternoon, and maybe an hour or two in the evening is all there is left to accomplish those core values. Next in the exercise, I want you to start time-blocking those core value responsibilities that you had with their associated percentage of time allotted. For example, if you stated that family was a core value and you gave it 30% weight then you need to find about a third of your time to block out responsibilities related to this. Taking your kids to school or a dentist appointment does not count as core value time. In another example, if you stated advocacy was a core value and you assigned it 20% weight then you should be reasonably setting aside a fifth of your time. The perspective of time is seven days a week in this exercise so maybe your advocacy time happens on the weekends or maybe it's a part of the business or work you do.

Time-blocking can quickly help you to prioritize your time and accomplish the things most important to you. Recall Abigail, the entrepreneur I worked with - she had a small business to close out and when I asked her what was stopping her from taking it off the list, she told me she needed about eight hours to get all the tasks done to close out the business. So I asked her to time block two hours on a Monday, four hours on a Saturday, and four hours the following week so that way within two weeks of our work session together she could see that list of responsibilities removed which would create more time for the things she wanted to be doing for her new business.

Carolyne was also someone who benefited from time-blocking and after I shared the technique with her, she was able to complete two successful non-profit fundraising events in addition to her full-time job. The best part was when she called me to tell me that she actually enjoyed herself at the fundraisers because she was so well prepared that everything went smoothly. Life does not have to be a non-stop rat race, or an anxiety-filled series of dreaded commitments. You can prioritize your time, protect it for the things you value, and still have all the hairs on your head. The example calendar I provide in this exercise was actually Carolyne's.

Time-blocking does have flexibility to it so do not feel like you are being placed in a rigid box. I will start my week out with 4-hour block to write a business plan or a 2-hour block to complete a doctorate paper in the evening. Once I get started on the project or task with no distractions, I find that I can usually get it done in half the time. Now the opposite can also happen. I may only allot myself an hour to accomplish a brief task and after getting started I realize I need more data or research to get it done.

My best advice to you is always to try and cushion your time blocks. It could be for traveling to and from a meeting, having time to gather more information, or so you can grab a snack along the way. Wouldn't you rather have an extra half hour or an hour back to yourself if you complete the task in less time, than feel the stress of needing to finish it on another day?

This technique is something you will need to try for at least a month to really get the muscle memory needed to sustain it. Experiencing the distractions and learning to cushion your time blocks take practice and trial and error. You also have many of your core value responsibilities that you listed were only weekly or monthly tasks, so you need to see at least a monthly view of your calendar. I would like you to carve out time in week one at the end of each day to reflect on how the time-blocking went for the day. Did you adhere to your schedule? If not, what got in the way and what do you need to do differently tomorrow? Its ok to make adjustments - just make sure you are not putting important tasks on the shelf or procrastinating on the goals you have set.

Starting in week two, I want you to block off time each Friday to reflect on how the time-blocking is going. The weekly practice of reflection is really important. You will find that you are initially surprised at how much you can accomplish with this technique and then you will find all the tasks you didn't quite complete and you can set the intention to time-block them the following week so they can get done.

Life happens so be forgiving of yourself if it takes some adjusting the first few weeks. When you have completed an entire month of true commitment to time-blocking and your core values a priority, you will find that your life changes. You will also notice the people in your life will change.

The *Fierce* individual who has made their core values part of their daily, weekly, and monthly life will start to see changes in their relationships.

The time-blocking technique is a form of external communication to others as they start to see your strategy come to life. The way in which you show up in each of these responsibilities will start to shift. When you are completing a task related to your core values you will find an inner joy that will resonate from within you.

When you start saying yes to yourself instead of saying yes to everyone else, you will also find people around you may negatively react to this positive change. Their expectations of you have been formed by their previous experiences with you, so naturally when the experiences change so will the need to adjust their expectations.

Carolyne had a few obstacles her first month. The first came with family who were very used to her taking on all the responsibilities of the home. After week two she started delegating some of the household chores to her children and spouse in order to level the load on her plate and to allow her more time for the advocacy work she was passionate about. Lots of gripes came from within the walls of her home, but very quickly the family saw how happy Carolyne was and this shifted the energy.

The second obstacle came as she was the event coordinating for her extended family celebrations and Carolyne decided to ask her sister to set up a family function so she could have time to plan her non-profit fundraiser. Her sister was actually excited to step in and do this, however the rest of the extended family was not used to anyone else coordinating family functions, so they gave Carolyne lots of grief. After a successful fundraiser and family anniversary party, the members of her extended family got to see this positive change in her and started to ask if she was taking a new medication. Carolyne laughed as she told me "they thought I was on drugs" and she knew the technique was making a huge impact in her life.

The first technique, and quite honestly the most difficult to integrate, is time-blocking as it takes intention and self-discipline. The next technique is the first impression you send out into the world without even being in the room – your resume. It amazes me how many people I come across who do not have a resume or have one that is decades old. This may have been the case for the generations that came before me; starting a job at 18 and then staying there until they retire. The world today has changed and even those legacy careers with one employer require a resume when you want to move up or take on a new position.

Resume

A resume is a powerful tool. It is the first step in obtaining the career you want. Now if you are an entrepreneur or a student and you are thinking, "I am not applying for any jobs, so I don't need a resume" then pay attention because resumes are not just used for job applications. What used to be considered a single piece of paper scribed in stone (just kidding) is now a several page document complete with your strengths, accomplishments, and relative educational and professional experience that make you desirable for a given position.

The position could in fact be a job or it could be a scholarship, internship, or ambassadorship if you are a student. As an entrepreneur, a resume can be requested by investors, clients, and employers you want to do business with. This important document is a quick summary of your knowledge, skills, and abilities (KSAs). It should answer the most basic of questions – why should they choose you?

You can find many samples, templates, and opinions on what should and should not be included in a resume on the internet. I am not here to critique the aesthetics except for to say crazy templates, fonts, and photos are just distractions. Save those for the PowerPoint presentation you need to pitch to an investor or the case study you need to share in a panel interview. The resume needs to be simple, easy to read, and concisely communicate key values, strengths, and accomplishments.

When recruiters are sourcing hundreds of resumes for one position you need to stand out in the crowd, but not in a **Bold Script** kind of way. Let your KSAs speak for themselves. Many companies use resume scanner software programs that look for key words as artificial intelligence continues to make HR functions more efficient.

In **Communication Exercise 3 – Part 2** (p. 71) you will find some key questions necessary to start building your position-specific resume. I do not believe in cookie-cutter resume templates. You know the one you can generate and apply for 25 online jobs with. It is impersonal at best and disingenuous at worse. You should have a position-specific resume which means that for each juncture where you desire for a change in your career, business, or journey, the resume should reflect that occasion.

A resume for an operational director role should look different than a resume for a non-profit Board of Directors' seat. A resume for a college scholarship should look different than one for an internship. Lastly a resume for a financial investor should look different than one for a client. Why they should choose you for each of these positions is different because the circumstances are different. Tailor your resume accordingly.

My first experience writing resumes came when I was fourteen years old and I was vying for a community ambassador role. The application questions were written in such a way that I did not realize at the time I was writing my first resume. And you want to know how I completed that lined application? On a typewriter – remember those?!

Okay, all jokes aside this first experience started opening up my eyes to my educational and volunteer experience which this youth organization was looking for in order to select their next ambassador. Why I wanted the role, what I had done in service of my community in the past, how I was investing in my education, and what opportunities I was taking part in to develop myself as a young leader were all critical components.

A few years later as I ambitiously sought to be the first person in my family to attend a four-year university, I developed a scholarship resume. This time I wanted the local, state, and national organizations

I was applying to for college funding to not only know why they should choose me, but how their investment in my education would pay dividends. I knew that I would always pay it forward, give back to my community, and seek out positive changes in the world with my education.

I also had the luxury at that time in my life of amazing mentors – my youth organization leader and my high school guidance counselor. They were both able to provide guidance, review, and feedback on these resumes and applications. I was determined to become an Orthopedic surgeon at this venture and thus was going to need to get into a great college in addition to needing lots of scholarships to pay for my education.

The key to a great resume is a clear and concise summary of your expertise and accomplishments. For each job you choose to highlight you should list 3-4 key responsibilities in bullet point form and then 3-4 accomplishments in that role below it (**see example**). Make sure to have a section highlighting your educational and professional associations and accomplishments. This may include but not be limited to memberships, conferences, certificates, degrees, and positions held. An important tip is to make sure and read the position description that you are applying to, the scholarship details, or the investor's profile so you can tailor your resume to the strengths that you possess that align to their specific needs. It is also a great idea when you are sharing accomplishments to use data.

If you can demonstrate a strength or skill with a quick data point, then the recipient of your resume doesn't have to just trust what you say but can have hard data to support it. This could be helping grow sales by 20%, increasing referrals by 10%, or maybe it's contributing 100 hours in service at a non-profit or raising $2,000. The power of numbers helps to strengthen the words in your resume. Be prepared to speak to these facts and figures if you get an interview. Never put a data point on your resume that you can't explain who, what, where, when, or how. You do not need to list every responsibility, accomplishment, skill, or organization you have ever been a part of. This is why I suggest tailoring your resume.

You can pick and choose the applicable experience you want to highlight in your resume without needing a chronological list of all you have done. You may find an employer/client will ask about gaps in time on your resume. This is perfectly acceptable and you can be prepared with a response about how that was a period of time in which you were developing skills and experience in another role, organization, or adventure that you did not feel aligned with the position you are now seeking. The older HR practices of chronological resumes have been replaced with the meaningful and concise resumes that speak to the position that is desired. Remember, this is the first impression you get without even being in the room!

Interview

Communicating who you are and what you value is never more important than in an interview. Most people find themselves with the extreme anxiety at this point in the process. There is a level of intimacy when being interviewed or even interviewing with a panel of people, that can cause even the most seasoned professionals to get nervous. It is my belief, however, that when an individual truly knows themselves, their core values, and their highlighted strengths, then any interview should feel as comfortable as having a conversation over coffee with a friend.

One of the most important things that I tell people when they are preparing for an interview is to remember this is a two-way conversation and thus a two-way relationship you are forming. The employer, client, organization you are interviewing with must in fact ask questions to get to know you, decide if you are the right fit, and ultimately select you for the position or opportunity you are seeking, but you are also in the driver seat and should be interviewing them to make sure their company aligns with your values.

Over the last few years, I have had the pleasure of interviewing high school students in my surrounding community as part of their sophomore or junior year curriculum. These are some of my most favorite days because for all of them it is the first time, they are interacting with a community member and getting to see what an interview feels like. Their teachers of course prepare them and teach lessons on writing their resumes, picking a job of interest to interview for, how to dress, make eye contact, shake hands, etc. The part that amazes me are the small handful of students that walk in that room and are so happy to be there. They have a joy about them that is contagious, and it is not because they have any more interview skills than their nervous and shy friend who proceeded them. These students know what they want, they have a goal, and they are excited to share it with me.

This year we did the interviews via Zoom as the school is on distance learning due to the pandemic. The students got to participate in a breakout session with two community members and have about ten minutes with us. The level of vulnerability and courage each of them showed was so impressive. These students are not only managing the demands of school at home, but helping care for siblings, work part-time jobs to help with the financial strains of their families, and finding new creative ways to still volunteer in their community.

They not only did a great job at their first interview, they learned new skills about how to do interviews virtually. There are many professionals who have still yet to experience what it's like to interview on a virtual platform. Taking into account technology glitches, what the background setting looks like, what you are dressed in, and how the lighting captures your expressions are not easy tasks to manage.

I also had the pleasure to teach a high school business class these very same interview tips I am going to share with you. The interview is your chance to go beyond what you shared in your resume and help them get to know you as an individual. To keep it simple I have made an easy **what to do and what to avoid** list for your reference (p. 65).

The first thing we should discuss is <u>what to avoid</u> when interviewing:

1. Not Being Prepared - Make sure you understand the position you are applying to, the organization, and any pertinent skills required.
2. Poor Communication - Speed, articulation, breath, nervous habits, and ambiguity are all things to be aware of.
3. Distractions - Having gum or mints, wrinkled attire, fidgeting with a pen, cell phone (turn it off).

Preparation is such a critical step and researching the organization you are seeking a position with, asking for investment in your business, or looking to partner with. Nervous habits get the best of everyone so know what your tendencies are and have a plan to mitigate them. If you are someone who talks fast (like me) then make sure you are conscious of your tempo, take breaths, and annunciate your words. If you are someone who gives yes or no answers when you are nervous, have examples and stories to tell written down in a notebook in front of you so you can easily reference them. If you are someone who says "um" or "like" this nervous habit can be overcome by practicing ahead of time, knowing your material, and taking conscious breaths before you speak. Lastly, if you fidget then find a comfortable place to lay your hands and avoid pen clicking, hair twisting, clothes pulling, and any other distraction.

Let us now talk about one of the biggest mistakes you can make in an interview these days. The physical way in which you show up leaves a lasting impression. They won't remember if you wore a pink blouse or a blue button-down however, they will remember if it was wrinkled, untucked, or torn. They also won't remember the portfolio or notebook you walk in with, but they will remember if you set your cell phone on the table. Leave the cell phone OFF! I promise you no major emergencies will happen in the 30-60 minutes you are in an interview and if you are worried about that leave the company's number with a loved one who can reach you there if that were to happen.

A cell phone on the desk or table says to the people taking their time to interview you that "you are not as important to me as whatever text or call I am waiting on." Then there is always the unintentional ringtone that plays loudly, and you swore you turned it to silent. Don't be that person in an interview – set the intention to bring your best self to the room with no distractions. Also, I should not even have to mention it, but please remove the gum or mints from your mouth beforehand. I have had too many interviews where I watched the person smack bright green gum and I could not hear anything they were saying.

Avoiding those three common pitfalls can truly help you feel comfortable and confident when interviewing. Now let me share my top three tips on how to ace your interview:

1. Know Your Audience - Do your homework on the organization and the person(s) interviewing you if at all possible and pay attention to the non-verbal in the room.
2. Communicate Your Value - Have examples prepared that highlight what you can bring to the position, the team, and the organization.
3. Leave a Lasting Impression - Your preparedness for the interview should shine from your printed resume to your attire and have questions for them.

Part of your research and preparation for the interview is to know the company, people, and position you are wanting to work for. When you get the call or email letting you know you are selected for an interview, it is ok to ask who you will be interviewing with. Do your best to look up the panel of people on the company's website, on LinkedIn, and search any professional organizations they may be associated with. This research will help you gain insight if these are the kind of people you want to work with. Remember it is about aligning your values.

The same research should be applied to the position. Read the job description and if not made available then ask HR for a copy in advance of your interview. Try to find people who current occupy that role or a similar one in the company and research them as well. Finally, when you get into the interview (virtual or in-person) make sure to read the room. Does it appear the people like their own job, are happy to work with one another, do they look attentive or distracted, do they seem annoyed or tired? Making a conscious effort to know your audience and be able to speak to each of them in a way that is engaging is important.

Think of your interview as a first date. You want to present your best self; physically, mentally, and emotionally. The decision to "date" this company needs to be mutual, enjoyable, and at the end of it you should both come away knowing one another better. If you find people in the room detached or distracted, ask yourself if you are presenting your authentic self and communicating your values effectively. If so, then ask yourself if you want to work with people who do not value your time or your commitment to the interview process.

Communicating your values should come easy to you now as you have gone through the strategic exercise of identifying them, prioritizing them, and making them apart of your everyday routine. Make sure to have examples of how you see yourself contributing to the position, the team, and the company. If it's an investor or client, then have data or stories to share on how their commitment to you will make a difference, generate a profit, or allow for innovation.

It is important to leave a lasting impression with your interview. Today's environment is very competitive, and we will talk more about this in the last section of this book, so you want to make sure you stand out in the crowd. One of the students I met in the interviews shared that his strength is his ambition, but it can also be his weakness as peers can see him as bossy. I shared with this young man I knew firsthand what that feels like and the lesson I learned the hard way was that ambition does not have to come at the expense of others. In fact, you can accomplish your goals and take others along with you – that's the sign of a true leader.

Sharing stories like this in an interview is powerful. First, it lets the company know you can recover from failure and learn lessons to improve. Second, sharing your vulnerabilities can create an authentic experience for everyone involved and it is when the guard is down that people truly see you. Finally, be inquisitive with the interviewer. It is highly recommended that you come with at least 2-3 questions of your own. This can leave the impression with the company that you were thoughtful enough to not only prepare but are genuinely interested in knowing more about the people and organization you are with in this experience.

Simon Sinek will tell you to start with your why and Brené Brown will tell you to take off your armor, I like all of their advice and I will add to it that having the courage of conviction is truly powerful. If you get halfway through an interview and realize this company has values that do not align with yours, then I challenge you to respectfully thank them for their time, the opportunity to discuss the role, and kindly walk away. You will save yourself months if not years of misery working for people or an organization that does not value what you do. Practice those values do not just profess them!

Interview Tips

What to Avoid	What to Do
Not Being Prepared *Make sure you understand the position you are applying to, the organization, and any pertinent skills required.*	**Know Your Audience** *Do your homework on the organization and the person(s) interviewing you if at all possible*
Poor Communication *Speed, articulation, breath, nervous habits, and ambiguity are all things to be aware of.*	**Communicate Your Value** *Have examples prepared that highlight what you can bring to the position, the team, and the organization*
Distractions *Having gum or mints, wrinkled attire, fidgeting with a pen, cell phone (turn it off)*	**Leave a Lasting Impression** *Your preparedness for the interview should shine from your printed resume to your attire and have questions for them*

Social Media and Marketing

The final section of communication is how you show up in this world and promote yourself. If you are a professional seeking a new position, then I highly suggest you open up Google and type in your name. See what comes up and go ahead and click on the links. I know it is scary to google yourself but trust me this is what hiring managers are doing before they interview you. The same goes if you are an entrepreneur or any business honestly, people are going to google you, so I highly suggest you know what they are seeing.

Your Facebook and LinkedIn profiles are going to be the most common place they will go to first. Secondly, they will visit company websites you are associated with, media stories you've been mentioned in, and look at any images or videos tied to your name. If you think you have the privacy settings all set up to avoid this from happening, let me burst your bubble. A profile picture is worth 1,000 words - especially if it appears to be a bar photo, swimwear photo, or poorly taken selfie. Do yourself a favor and get a headshot taken.

Your professionally photo should appear almost exclusively everywhere you can be marketed as this sets your brand and I will make one small exception for a personal Facebook page, however, if you choose a family photo or selfie, make sure you keep it classy.

The imagery you put out into social media allows people to judge you before thy know you. However, if chosen correctly, it can leave them with a positive impression and desire to get to know you further. Your values should be clearly communicated in these platforms as well. From the headers you choose, the quotes you share in your bio, and the organizations and people you choose to associate yourself with. Sharing a politically charged post publicly on your social media can invite future clients, employers, and colleagues to make value judgements about you that could prevent further opportunities. There is a professional way to be an advocate of issues important to you.

When it comes to marketing yourself or your business, these core values will be the key to your success. See the **social media and marketing tips** on page 73. As Simon shared in an earlier section, he does not do business with others who do not share his values and you may find the same to be true of others who choose to be your customers, clients, or colleagues. The best marketing you can have today is an authentic message that is aligned to your core values and shows up in every decision you make. Your resume is a marketing tool, your interview is a marketing tool, the social media you participate in is a marketing tool, and the way you show up virtually and in-person for interactions with others is a marketing tool.

Have you ever heard the story of the CEO everyone adored at work, who had great professional management of his social media and public relations, but was caught on video outside a grocery store in a verbal and physical altercation that left his reputation tarnished? You are always marketing yourself. The *Fierce* people you know in your life are not just that way from 9-5 p.m. nor do they only align their values while at work.

Remember being *Fierce* means being *intimately aware of one's purpose, values, strengths, and dreams such that the journey is filled with an intense passion for life.* In the CEO's case, maybe his passion got the better of him. But remember that marketing is all about authenticity.

Communication is the third technique in developing your *Fierce* strategy and now that you have learned tools and tips for how to time-block, write your resume, interview, and manage your social media and marketing, I want you to write down four goals.

One communication goal for each of the four areas that you can accomplish in the next month.

Maybe it is updating your resume to include tangible accomplishments or maybe its committing to practice with a friend or family member on your interview skills. You could clean up your social media or build out a professional profile and commit to marketing yourself or your business in all of your authentic behaviors. This is the longest section as it is extremely important to externally communicate your fierceness and start owning the journey that you desired to start when you picked up this book.

If any of the parts in **Exercise 3** brought about questions, anxieties, or confusion this is where my available consulting may be the right answer for you. I am available for a free thirty-minute call to review any of your needs and evaluate how I can help. Simply email yourfiercestrategy@gmail.com and know you are not alone in this process. Time to take another deep breath in and exhale out.

What is your strategy and how are you going to start communicating it?

Communication Exercise 3 - Part 1

	Sun	Mon	Tue	Wed	Thu	Fri	Sat
6:00 am		AM	AM	AM	AM	AM	
7:00 am		Routine	Routine	Routine	Routine	Routine	
8:00 am		Emails	Emails	Emails	Emails	Emails	
9:00 am							
10:00am							
11:00am							
12:00pm		Lunch	Lunch	Lunch	Lunch	Lunch	
1:00 pm							
2:00 pm							
3:00 pm							
4:00 pm							
5:00 pm							
6:00 pm		PM	PM	PM	PM	PM	
7:00 pm		Routine	Routine	Routine	Routine	Routine	
8:00 pm							
9:00 pm							

Time-Blocking Example

	Sun	Mon	Tue	Wed	Thu	Fri	Sat
6:00 am		AM	AM	AM	AM	AM	F
7:00 am		Routine	Routine	Routine	Routine	Routine	U
8:00 am	Clean	Emails	Emails	Emails	Emails	Emails	N
9:00 am	House						D
10:00am		Work	Work	Work	Work	Work	R
11:00am	Brunch						A
12:00pm		Lunch	Lunch	Lunch	Lunch	Lunch	I
1:00 pm	Nap	Work	Work	Work	Work	Work	S
2:00 pm							E
3:00 pm	E	Kids	Kids	Kids	Kids	Kids	R
4:00 pm	V	Work	Work	Work	Work	Work	
5:00 pm	E						
6:00 pm	N	Soccer	Karate	Event P	Dance	Movie	
7:00 pm	T	PM	PM	PM	PM	PM	Date
8:00 pm		Routine	Routine	Routine	Routine	Routine	Night
9:00 pm		Event Planning and Preparation					

70

Communication Exercise 3 – Part 2

Resume Building

1. What type of resume is it going to be?
   a. Job/Role
   b. Scholarship
   c. Investor/Client
   d. Other

2. What is your experience?
   This should be relative to the type of resume

3. What have you accomplished in each of your listed experience areas?
   Provide data or examples

4. What education or professional development have you had relative to this resume?
   Degrees, internships, certificates, conferences, seminars, workshops

5. What are your professional affiliations/honors?
   Memberships, Roles Held, Awards, Publications

6. What additional experience do you have?
   This is where you can list other jobs or experience not relative to this specific resume but still roles or jobs held

7. What are your volunteer commitments?
   Organizations, events, causes supported

8. Who are your references?
   List relative contacts for the resume type

Resume Example

Professional Experience

Position ABC
Company XYZ   **Month Year – Current Role**

- o Responsibility 1
- o Responsibility 2
- o Responsibility 3

Accomplishments in Role

- o Example with Data 1
- o Example with Data 2
- o Example with Data 3

Educational and Professional Development

Degree
University ABC   **Year**

Certification
Organization XYZ   **Year**

Professional Affiliations and Honors

Organization Membership   **Year**
Organization Award   **Year**
Publication   **Year**

Additional Experience

Position Held/Organization   **Year**
Position Held/Organization   **Year**

Volunteer Commitments

Organization/Event/Cause   **Year**
Organization/Event/Cause   **Year**

References
Relative Contact for Type of Resume

Social Media & Marketing

What to Avoid	What to Do
Unprofessional Profile Photo *Make sure you to avoid selfies, college bar photos, and inappropriately dressed pictures*	**Professional Profile** *Have a nice headshot taken, utilize a headline, robust bio, and clear concise messaging*
Publicly Sharing Political or Controversial Posts *Choose wisely what you advocate for and the information you share*	**Communicate Your Values** *Your core values should be evident within 1 minute of viewing your social media or marketing materials*
Inconsistent Branding *Make sure all platforms have the same messaging, profile photo, and you are aware of the purpose of each technique you are using*	**Meaningful Connections** *Associate yourself with others whose values align and know who you have connected to your network*

Collaboration

"Fight for the things that you care about, but do it in a way that will lead others to join you" – Ruth Bader Ginsberg

----

Truly *Fierce* individuals want to enjoy the journey with others - they understand the value of human connection, and they want to bring others along for the ride. This year – 2020 – definitely challenged our traditional ways of collaborating as we had to safely create physical distance between us and minimize any large groups in order to prevent the spread of the virus. Large associations had to cancel conferences while others had the time to reimagine their seminars and workshops in virtual ways. The one big takeaway from a conference is the ability to network with others and for those organizations who created virtual content and conferences – overcoming the networking options was more challenging.

The one thing 2020 did do for us, however, was show the power of a movement - the *Fierce* individuals who used their voices to bring awareness and advocate for change. I love the RBG quote as her passing inspired a whole new generation of women to speak up and fight for their rights. All of the tragedy of this year also showed us the power of our human connection. The commitment to diversity, equity, and inclusion became a top priority for organizations across our globe and while it existed before 2020, it never received the true resources and dedication needed to make the necessary changes. We still have a ways to go, but the collaboration amongst individuals from all races, ethnic groups, genders, ages, and socioeconomic statuses inspires me every day.

"We don't have to do all of it alone. We were never meant to." – Brené Brown

If you have been feeling all alone in this world or overwhelmed by all of the responsibilities on your plate, it is ok to ask for help, to reach out and connect. It is great to have your inner circle of close friends you trust, to have coaches, mentors, and individuals who can support you, and it can also be greatly rewarding to give your time to others; each of these can cure the loneliness and bring meaning in your life. Michelle Obama, our absolutely *Fierce* and inspiring first lady said, "We should always have three friends in our lives. One who walks ahead who we look up to and follow; one who walks beside us, who is with us every step of our journey; and then, one who we reach back for and bring along after we've cleared the way." As you think about building or improving your network you should consider all three layers.

When people hear the word networking they think of schmoozing, rubbing elbows with others, collecting contacts, connections, or business cards. These old paradigms about networking have been challenged by the power of social networking sites like LinkedIn or Facebook. The true purpose of networking is to build relationships. In this section of the book, we are going to dive into the benefits and how-tos of networking as well as the important relationship-building techniques. As I described earlier, getting a job or an interview can happen simply for your connection to someone either at that organization or a relationship with someone you know who has a connection with that organization. A network is also not just about the professional benefits.

Networking has the potential to enrich your life in ways you never thought possible. Through the power of networking, I have had the opportunities to travel, garner a fellowship, receive new career opportunities, and meet some of my favorite people on this planet. Networking also helps you to find more of "your people" - the ones whose values align with yours and who you can work with, support, and enjoy the journey with. The **top tips for networking** (p. 79) include improving your current state, attracting future opportunities, and a lifelong pathway of learning, growing and succeeding. In order to begin networking or expanding your existing network, you must set the intention and overcome any fears about putting yourself out there. The investment you make in building your network should be a continual effort that will in turn pay dividends for many years to come. Like any relationship, it requires ongoing nurturing and energy. The true word of mouth reputation building that can come from networking can build your business or career connections in a much faster way than any paid for marketing. Attending a networking event is a lot like dating - you want to bring your authentic self and yet you are filled with nerves and anxiety about who and where you will meet. The handshake is like the first date and then I see a lot of people try to go right to getting married as the first thing they share is their sales pitch: convincing this newly made connection to buy their product, enroll in their program, or help them get a new job. This is a big mistake and you must "go slow to go fast" as one of my old bosses used to say.

Building a relationship and maintaining one are two distinct actions and networking requires the same methods. Just like there are six C's to your *Fierce* strategy plan, there are **six key tactics** to a great collaboration and networking strategy:

1. Be good at connecting with a few key associations, groups, or organizations that align with your core values

2. Be an active participant and authentic in your interactions (virtual or in-person)

3. Give first before you ask for something
4. Plan to be fully present at events – no distractions, commit to the entire length of the event, no multitasking
5. Maintain existing relationships and make time for new ones
6. Dedicate time in your calendar for following up with connections, promised referrals, or new groups you want to connect with

Networking Tips

Improvement	Tip
Current State	Set the intention to begin networking and pick a few key organizations or platforms to begin immediately that align with your core values
Future Opportunities	Give first and help others make connections, referrals, and mentorship – then you will find opportunities will come back to you for career, business, and new personal connections
Lifelong Pathways	Maintain relationships, participate in ongoing personal growth and development activities, and maintain loyalty with aligned organizations

Whether or not you are an extrovert or an introvert, you can make a plan to create and maintain a successful network that does not have to riddle you with anxiety. First, decide how you want to show up - everything from what you want to wear, to what kind of materials you may bring are important planning steps. If the event is virtual make sure to get your contact information into the chat box right away and also decide where your background will be as it can either invite people to want to interact with you or it can deter them.

My suggestion is to find a real place to be sitting on virtual events and while Zoom may not appreciate that I am suggesting to avoid their fun backgrounds, it is my opinion that seeing someone in their real environment is part of bringing your authentic self to the platform. Imagine walking into a live in-person networking event with a poster in front of you displaying a beach and there is a small cut out for your head - how authentic is that?

Similar to what I shared in the interview section, make sure you are presentable. We have all heard the stories of someone in a great shirt who has to stand up for some reason during a virtual call only to reveal the pajama bottoms they still have on or even worse their underwear. Even when an event is virtual you should put forth the effort that you would for an in-person event, and you will find that it changes your energy level as well. One tip – do not show up to a virtual event and keep your camera off. No one wants to interact with just audio and a picture of your dog.

Let's talk about commitment for a moment. The difference between your standard social media and your social network is the value of the relationship and commitment. You can choose to like, follow, subscribe, and connect with hundreds of organizations and professionals which can make your LinkedIn and Facebook appear to have a vast network. How many of those connections have a two-way working relationship?

The same can be said for friends. You can have hundreds of people you call friends, but how many of them would you say are genuinely and authentically relationships that both parties find value in? A more realistic view can be that you have hundreds of acquaintances, colleagues, and past friendships that you still are connected to through social media, but you only have a smaller group of true friends. The maturity that comes with the experience of managing relationships over time is how you can discern the differences.

As I suggest in the first tactic, pick a few key associations, groups, or organizations that align with your core values and commit to becoming a part of their network. Now, these chosen few can change over time, but do not try to be everything to everyone and over-commit yourself to twenty organizations. This will stretch your time and energy out, cause eventual burnout, and not bring meaningful connections to your life. I am the queen of multitasking, so take it from me - the more you try to do at any one given time, the less you are actually bringing your authentic self to any relationship.

Now Abigail, who I talked about earlier in this book, is the queen of connection and she truly has a gift for maintaining meaningful relationships and connections with hundreds of people but she is the exception to the rule as it is her life's purpose - her true gift and the source of her entrepreneurial spirit. Carolyne, as you can recall, was like most of us and felt that she was only giving 30 percent to a bunch of people instead of 100 percent to a smaller few. If we want that true committed and meaningful benefit of a network, we have to be selective about where we spend our time and energy.

While it is important to focus on a few key groups, it is also important to focus while participating in these networking events, platforms, and conversations. If you commit to attending a live or virtual event, time-block it and do not try to be multitasking while you are there. It is distracting to others, breaks away from your authenticity, and gives an impression that you are not truly committed or have better things to do. I suggest turning the cell phone off or on airplane mode, avoiding scrolling on platforms while also trying to virtually network, and staying for the entirety of the event – some of the best networking happens before and after the event actually starts.

This year I have had to host a few board and strategy retreats and I found the most value in the morning coffee or the evening happy hour. People are less guarded, more authentic, and deeper conversations happen when you are having a meal or a drink and can intimately connect. I was also an attendee at a few virtual conferences this fall, and I enjoyed the new technology platforms that allowed for actual networking break out rooms.

One organization actually used a five-minute matching system and over the course of 45 minutes, I met nine different people – it almost felt like speed dating. The other conference had small group virtual rooms where 4-5 people could meet and talk over their virtual platform and gave us all the professional topic of the do's and don'ts of your LinkedIn profile which allowed for some great sharing.

Let us put some of these tips into practice. In **Collaboration Exercise 4 – Part 1** (p. 86) I want you to detail out the three organizations, groups, or associations you plan to collaborate and network with over the next 12 months. Utilizing your notebook, next to each one I would like you to put which of your core values that group aligns with. Beneath the selected organization, research which networking events, platforms, and key stakeholders you will connect with, attend, or participate in and list by when. This is part of your *Fierce* strategy to commit to collaborating so more people can get to know this amazing new you and what you are all about.

As you start to participate in these groups, I want you to use **Collaboration Exercise 4 – Part 2** (p. 87) to capture down the authentic connections you make. Who are the people that make the organization worth staying connected to? What are the values they share with you? What can you offer them – coaching, mentoring, referrals, other connections, friendship? What can they offer you? How will you maintain your relationship? As you begin building this network you want to be purposeful about those you give your time and energy to as you recall in section three, your time and resources are limited and maintaining this new relationship will require time-blocking!

Finally, in **Collaboration Exercise 4 – Part 3** (p. 88), I want you to capture three months, six months, and one year into these newly formed networks how they have helped your strategy. This is the time for reflection so as you build the new annual strategy for the following year, you can make decisions on whether to stay committed to that relationship/network or to find a new one to build from.

Remember your Fierce strategy is a living and ongoing commitment to yourself and reflecting on choices you make today and how they impact you down the road is important for ongoing continuous improvement. You may find these chosen networks helped you to build your business, get a new job, travel somewhere, or taught you something about yourself.

The power of collaborating and building your network is also about the service to others. Recall what Michelle Obama said, "One who we reach back for and bring along after we've cleared the way." As you send the first few months in these new networks, try to identify someone who you can help as well. Mentoring and helping others along the way is so rewarding and can drive new personal growth and skills for you in relationship building. Try to recall the things you loved about a previous coach or mentor as well as the things you do not like and share those stories with your new connection. Bring the vulnerability to your connection and find ways in which you can enrich their lives. The passion for life you will find as you commit to your own Fierce strategy will inspire others to do the same.

If any of the parts in **<u>Exercise 4</u>** brought about questions, anxieties, or confusion this is where my available consulting may be the right answer for you. I am available for a free thirty-minute call to review any of your needs and evaluate how I can help. Simply email yourfiercestrategy@gmail.com and know you are not alone in this process. Time to take another deep breath in and exhale out.

Making connections with others and building relationships in order to increase your network is more rewarding than taxing and living your *Fierce* strategy will attract more people to your network.

Collaboration Exercise 4 – Part 1

Networking Organization or Platform	Aligned Core Values
1ˢᵗ Goal: What: With Who: By When:	
2ⁿᵈ Goal: What: With Who: By When:	
3ʳᵈ Goal: What: With Who: By When:	

Collaboration Exercise 4 – Part 2

Authentic Connection	Follow-Up
Name: Shared Values: Give: Receive:	*Plan to maintain connection – could be call, email, scheduled event, etc. Make sure to add this into time-blocking*
Name: Shared Values: Give: Receive:	
Name: Shared Values: Give: Receive:	
Name: Shared Values: Give: Receive:	
Name: Shared Values: Give: Receive:	

Collaboration Exercise 4 – Part 3

Authentic Connection	3 months	6 months	1 Year
Contact	How have they helped your strategy?	Are they continuing to help your strategy?	Do you want to maintain connection in the next strategy?
Name:			
Name:			
Name:			
Name:			
Name:			

Creativity

"Just try new things. Don't be afraid.

Step out of your comfort zones and soar,

alright?" – Michelle Obama

You have made it through four of the six C's in your *Fierce* strategy! You now have clarity of your values, a coordinated plan for how your responsibilities align with those values, a tangible guide to communicating your strategy through calendaring, your resume, your interview skills, and your social media and marketing, and finally a way to maximize the collaboration in your life to live those values in everything you do. Now for my favorite part – getting creative. Most people who judge me assume that all of the analytical and academic work that I do makes me a practical and boring nerd. While I embrace the nerdiness of my personality, I am at the very core a creative.

I need to bring you up to speed on my story as everything I am going to share with you afterward will make so much more sense. I grew up color coding letters that I wrote in a different pen for each line (and not just because it was a fad at that time). The walls of my childhood bedroom were covered in photo collages that I handmade and posters of people and things that I loved. I am not sure you could even see an inch of the purple wall paint I had behind them. I would rearrange the furniture in my room about every six months as well as the wall art which my parents – more specifically my stepdad – would laugh at the pushpin holes I had all over as this is how I hung things back then (before command strips were invented).

I was a typical child of the '80s. I had a Disco and R&B mom, a Hairband and Madonna dad, a classic rock stepdad, and my loving grandparents who raised me that honored the classic sounds of country music. I loved all of it! I would sing and dance for anyone who was willing to watch. At five and six I was throwing neighborhood talent shows in my back yard and recording "Grandpa Tell Me 'Bout the Good Ol Days" in a sound booth at Great America.

I started cheerleading for a local youth football team in town when I was eight, but my love for dance started at a small studio in town where I took ballet and jazz prior to cheer. I spent the next decade of my life dancing, choreographing, competing, and performing in every venue you could imagine. From an Oakland A's halftime to a K-Mart parking lot – I have danced in every type of atmosphere. When I was in high school, I got my first choreographer gig with a local singing group. I helped them with their shows, hired back up dancers, and choreographed all the dances for over two years. We toured the Central Valley from fair grounds to theaters and I found my passion. By the time I was a senior, I was awarded the opportunity to dance in the Paris New Year's Day parade. This was Y2K so everyone was freaking out about the world ending, but I fundraised my butt off so I could go and experience my first passport stamp. I also had a love for writing and photography. I was editor-in-chief of my school newspaper and helped with photos for the yearbook. I had a blast in leadership designing rallies, school dances, and any cultural or service-related festivals – I was at the helm. Homecoming each year was probably my favorite as we had an amazing class who went all out with our theme each year and would have 60-80 kids in full costume and choreography performing in the gymnasium or quad throughout the week. Needless to say, my creative spirit did not stop with my childhood.

I went onto pursue my academic dreams of being an orthopedic surgeon but made sure to minor in dance. I was in San Diego surrounded by culture and arts as I had never experienced before. I attended every dance show, theater production, and then off-Broadway ticket I could afford. When tragedy struck my family during my junior year of college, I made the decision to forgo the pursuit of medical school and swapped my major and minor.

I spent my last 18 months of college as a Theatre and Dance major working for one of the dance companies in town and soaking in all the creative I could. I just wanted to feel that joy forever and not the grief of losing my brother. He was a creative genius – he could play any instrument, write music, design computer programs, and at the same time solve complex calculus. He inspires me every day to keep being *Fierce*.

After graduating from college, growing up, and getting a "real job," I was able to put my finance and accounting skills to good use. All that science and math for pre-med still paid off, but this time for business. I dreamed every day though of becoming a world-famous choreographer or a backup dancer for Janet Jackson. I even started my application for grad school at UNC Greensboro for their Masters in Choreography. Sadly, I never turned it in because my other grown-up dreams of getting married and being an amazing housewife were coming true. I loved to cook and came from a long line of amazing chefs on my dad's side of the family. My husband didn't mind it at all as the poor guy couldn't boil water and he also had an amazing mother who cooked and baked phenomenal recipes.

After a little time settling into North Carolina, decorating and designing our first home, and trying to cultivate a green thumb (I was not successful at that), I found dance again. I went to a local dance studio and applied to teach. I had so much fun with 5 to 6-year old's taking some of their first ballet classes and then 13 to 14-year old's in my jazz class. I was a happy camper and could balance my accounting day job with my creative evenings.

Soon, I became a momma and my beautiful Grace Madelyn consumed my every breath. Creativity was found in tea parties, "happy day" cake, and lots of dress-up. Mommy and Me gymnastics, her first ballet, jazz, and tap classes, and countless hours watching her pretend to be Rachel Ray at her play kitchen.

As most moms do, I got wrapped up in what made her happy and even the hobbies and passions of my spouse, that I stopped having creative outlets for myself. The 2008-2009 economy crash and its impacts, ended up relocating us back to Northern California where I was born and raised. Being near family at the time was important and I simply dug in to survive the transition in life. I applied my business experience to healthcare and found a new passion as my journey had come full circle - from wanting to be a surgeon to now working in the administrative side of the health industry.

Slowly but surely my creativity found its way back. I would plan fun pharmacy week celebrations with mini talent shows and skits. I got back involved with a youth organization that shaped my young adolescence and became their Entertainment Director and then Competition Director. I was starting to feel like myself again.

Life brought along its own hardships and obstacles – a miscarriage then a divorce after the birth of my son Grant Montgomery, depression, and the financial strain of supporting myself and my babies. I knew I had to find something to pull myself out and I decided to go back to school and get my master's in business administration. I wanted to explore healthcare administration and move beyond administrative roles and into a leadership position. I needed to feel connected to my purpose and provide a pathway in which my future and my children's future could be more secure.

I worked fulltime, went to school at night for two years straight with no breaks, and we did what any other sacrificing family does – ate a lot of mac and cheese and PB&J. The dust settled on all of the personal life stuff and co-parenting became easier to do. We took our kids on vacations together, showed up for their soccer games and dance recitals, and life was finally turning around.

I accepted my first leadership role just two months after graduating with my master's degree and immediately found a passion for life again. I had a passion for my kids, my family, and my job, but this was finally a passion for my own dreams. One of the goals I had was to travel abroad solo as my reward for finishing the MBA, I went to Ireland on what I called "Eat, Pray, Love, and Drink." It was the best thing I have ever done for myself. I spent one week traveling between Dublin and Cork, seeing every town the movie 'P.S. I Love You' talked about (it's my favorite, what can I say I am a sucker for Gerard Butler). I finally had let go of my fear of being alone. It was true freedom being in another country, solo, with green fields for as far as the eye could see.

That same year, Sheryl Sandberg, Facebook COO and best-selling author of Lean In and later Option-B, launched a campaign. "Don't let yourself off the hook by deciding something is out of your reach, instead, ask yourself, 'What would I do if I weren't afraid?'" she said in her *If U Weren't Afraid Campaign*. It was specifically focused on women, who when they graduate college, do not have the same opportunities as men. At a young age when boys lead, they are applauded whereas when little girls lead, they are called "bossy" and this further is culturized as they grow up. Young girls are told to be polite, sweet, kind, and not too outspoken, A young man can be aggressive and ambitious and is labeled a leader, but women who do the same are called a "bitch." I strongly associated with these messages as I was told my entire childhood I was bossy, bitchy, too much for most people, not enough for the ones that I thought mattered, and as an adult "sit down and shut up" or "sit there and look pretty" messages were prevalent.

The campaign had something else that stood out for me. In fear you have two choices – **F**uck **E**verything **A**nd **R**un or **F**ace **E**verything **A**nd **R**ecover. I came back from Ireland with a newfound passion to stop apologizing for who I am, what I value, and what my goals were. I started to respectfully rebel against the male bosses who kept telling me to lower my hand, wait to speak, and stop taking the air out of the room. I no longer let those close to me have their narcissistic powers and I decided how to live my life no longer seeking their approval or opinion. What was so interesting is that while I definitely offended a few and pissed others off, I started to see the cheerleader section of my stadium grow. As I embraced my *Fierce*, other amazing people came into my life.

Then I found Brené who shared with me, "vulnerability is the birthplace of innovation, creativity, and change." As I started braving my wilderness, so many more things came into my life. I bought my first home on my own, remarried, had another son Dylan Grey, got promoted (three times), traveled the world - some trips with my kids or spouse, and some trips alone, and helped my partner go back to school, get his bachelor degree and his dream job.

I got really involved both, in my work and in my personal life, with oncology services and professional and philanthropic organizations that were improving the cancer patient's experience. I also became an advocate for March for Babies as my third pregnancy was high risk and I spent 7 days in the NICU with my 35-week preemie. The servant leader, that was shaped by my early days in a youth service organization, was now in full *Fierce* mode.

This time when I faced hardships and obstacles like another divorce and all the financial setbacks that come with losing half of the shit you worked so hard to build – I chose to **F**ace **E**verything **A**nd **R**ecover. I never wanted my story to include to failed marriages, but I realized how much both of my ex-husbands and I grew as a result of it. I am sure they would agree with me that we are all so much stronger as individuals for having experienced the love, pain, and growth that came from those relationships. We have three beautiful children, all get along great, and now you know why I am Amber Adams-Dixon-Campbell. I honor my family, my children, and my journey by embracing the names I have collected along the way.

I decided to go after another big dream – this time to teach business and travel the world while doing it. At the start of 2020, I began a Doctorate in Business Administration program, as I am passionate about the gender disparities in business leadership and want to further research the topic as part of my dissertation. What my academic pursuits have taught me – from BA to now DBA – is that knowledge is only as useful as the endeavors you apply it to.

Today I use my creativity to write engaging PowerPoints, business plans, and make unique gifts and experiences for my co-workers and colleagues. I still have walls of my home covered in art, photography, and creative signs. My love for travel influences the art in and around me every day and I still use different color pens on my dry erase board as I map out my plans. I know that being creative has helped me to be productive at work and in life.

You may think of creativity and productivity as opposites because being productive uses the left brain (methodical, organized, and logical) while being creative uses the right brain (intuitive, emotional, artistic). Have you ever seen the spinning ballerina? This mental exercise is supposed to help you see if you are more inclined to right-brain thinking or left-brain thinking. However, for me, I can see her turn both ways – initially, I am the right brain and then the left.

I believe creativity and productivity should be paired for meaningful connection and balance. Learning creative skills can help you in your job, business, and life and open your eyes to other perspectives increasing your energy and bringing you joy. These skills can start to facilitate into leadership, innovation, and courage, which are critical pieces of productivity.

Creativity can take the shape of vision boards, mind mapping, journaling, and any activity that involves coloring outside of the traditional lines. Your mind is able to travel to other places when you are being creativity. I know when I am driving down the road listening to my favorite music, I am creating dance pieces in my mind. The daydreaming you catch yourself doing at work is a great thing and you should capture it on a dream board or in a journal. Creativity is where we find inspiration and innovation.

Creativity is an investment in yourself – give your self-permission to explore, dream, and envision.

You will find that being around other creatives can sometimes help this process. Creative activities can also be a part of your collaborating and networking strategy. Finding others with similar values who want to also explore creative ventures like traveling to new places, trying new foods, learning a new hobby like painting, all can be great ways to collaborate and also fulfill your creative outlet.

In **Creativity Exercise 5** (p. 103) see a list of creative tips that you can incorporate into your strategic plan. Make sure to carve out time for these creative expressions or add them to your strategic goals. Pick at least three things from the list that you want to try and incorporate into your daily routine and write them down. Assign a timeline by when you will execute of each of them and then share these creative goals with someone in your new network so you can have an accountability partner.

1. Play music while working, exercising, cooking, relaxing, or driving. Try different kinds of music to support different kinds of atmospheres. Uplifting music while drudging through a project, dance music while exercising, classical music while relaxing, you get the point.

2. Allow yourself to daydream – just make sure to capture these amazing feelings, ideas, and inspirations somewhere you can see them (not just in your mind).

3. Travel and find your favorite place in nature. Go to new places, find a serene outdoor space, and experience new cultures.

4. Try new things – new food, new hobbies, new adventures. This is my top creative recommendation because when you stop living in your past or the nostalgia of your life you can create new experiences and memories that move your forward (at least Jay Shetty says so in *Think Like a Monk*).

5. Keep using creativity to reinvent yourself or continuously improve. The fact that you picked this book up and are well over a hundred pages in means that you are committed to self-improvement. Make visual maps of your life, dream boards of your future, and get to writing your own story or book!

6. Figure out what motivates you creatively and what does not. For me, dance and music bring out my creativity and I do not get the same energy from drawing or coloring, so I know this

is my best outlet. Find yours and incorporate it more in your life. I am dreaming of the day I can go back to another concert – live music is one of my favorite things!

When you complete the final section of this book, I want you to take all of the notes you have written and all the exercises you have completed to make a new board for your *Fierce* strategy. If you don't have a board then get a large piece of paper and fold it into six sections (in half and then in thirds). I want to see your six C's of your strategy come to life.

Those of you who take this challenge, finish the book, and send me a copy of your plan will receive a **free 60-minute strategic coaching session** with me. Send a photo of your board or poster to yourfiercestrategy@gmail.com or add #yourfiercestrategy to your brave and courageous social media post of the board. Once more, it's time to take another deep breath in and exhale out - your creative *Fierce* genius is going to emerge.

Creativity Exercise 5

Creative Tips to Incorporate
Play or Listen to Music
Daydream
Travel / Explore
Try New Things
Visual Maps / Dream Boards
Find New Motivations
Create New Experiences / Memories
Journal / Blog / Write
Coloring / Drawing / Paint
Photography
Theatre

Competitive Advantage

"As soon as I accomplish one thing, I just set a higher goal. That's how I've gotten to where I am." — Beyoncé

The final section of your *Fierce* strategy is knowing your competitive advantage. How are you different than those you are competing with? It may be the person you go up against for a promotion, another business in your same market, another entrepreneur with the same service to offer, or even another individual in your network competing for the time, energy, or resource of a colleague you find valuable. How do you set yourself apart and what makes you or your product more valuable than the next person?

Some of the things to think about if you own a business or are planning to start one are the products, services, reputation, location, and marketing of your company and how they compare to others in the same space. Some things to think about if you are going for the next level in your career are your knowledge, skills, and abilities and how they compare to the other candidate vying for that same role. You must get clear on what you are bringing to the table.

One of the original strategy tools for helping companies understand their competitive advantage is a SWOT analysis. Strengths, Weaknesses, Opportunities, and Threats. I believe the tool is applicable not just for businesses but individuals as well. In that high school business class that I shared interview tips with, I also shared how doing a SWOT before going into an interview can help you be prepared.

Its interview 101 that they will ask what your strengths and weaknesses are. How many teachers or coaches have told you to spin your weakness as really a strength? The concept is tired and as someone who has conducted hundreds of interviews, I can clearly see through the cookie-cutter answers. I challenged the students instead to really think about the internal and external qualities, responsibilities, skills, and abilities they possess.

In **Competitive Advantage Exercise 6 Part 1** (p. 114) you will find a SWOT analysis and proceeding it **two examples**. One for a business and one for an individual. I want you to complete this for yourself first and if you are in business or going to start one then complete the second one as well. The first step is to think internally about your own strengths and weaknesses. These are the things that you or your company do really well or don't do well. Do not confuse 'areas of opportunity for improvement' as something that should move to the O box – those are internal things within your control and are in fact weaknesses for the sake of this exercise. When you move down to the opportunities and threats, I want you to think externally to yourself or your business. You have less control but rather more influence in these areas.

In the student example, an opportunity might be taking a new class to learn a skill or getting involved in a sport or community organization. These opportunities exist to build new strengths. As a business, an opportunity might be to recruit new talent or invest in technology, again in order to build the strengths of your business. Threats are much harder for most people to work through. These are the external forces working against you.

When I taught the high school students, I shared with them a threat when applying for a job could be their existing commitments to school, family, and sports. These can limit the time and energy available to take on new employment or learn new skills. Individuals need to think about what barriers could prevent them from the opportunities they listed.

As a business, threats come in the form of your competitors who seek to gain the market share you are also trying to serve. A threat can also be technology if your business model has not incorporated its use. One example in business where people will confuse a weakness and a threat is when it comes to financial investment. Having a lack financial sustainability is a weakness because as the business you can control what is sold, what expenses you incur, and ultimately what the net proceeds are. Yet, a lack of financial investment can be a threat if seeking loans or investors is limited by the economy or other competitors.

One of the strongest competitive advantages you have is leveraging the knowledge, expertise, and talent of the people your hire. Having them do a SWOT exercise at the time of hire, during an annual review, or before a big project could be a helpful tool for their own personal growth and development, but also for your ability to leverage the right people at the right time for the right type of work. I recommend utilizing this SWOT exercise annually as part of your *Fierce* strategy planning. Once you can see all four areas, you can start to design goals and action plans to enhance your strengths, improve your weakness, take advantage of your opportunities, and mitigate your threats.

In **Competitive Advantage Exercise 6 Part 2** (p. 117) you will find seven different types of strategies for creating your competitive advantage. I encourage you to select at least one for yourself and one for your business to incorporate over the next year. Cost Strategy is making sure you have priced your product or service at a rate that consumers will pay. You can look at these two ways. First, if you want to beat out the competition, always monitor for a price right at or below them (think of WalMart's strategy). Second, you can price yourself above the market if you clearly communicate why your product or service is worthy of that cost (think of higher quality, faster service, more convenience, things people are willing to pay more for).

Operational Strategy is doing business in a more efficient or effective way than your competitors – this is where Amazon came in and killed the market and if you have ever seen the inside of one of their warehouses you will know why. Delivering a product same day or the next day when you competitors take days or weeks to do the same is a significant operational advantage.

The next strategy became very important this year – Flexibility. Individuals and Companies that can adapt quickly and move nimbly through change can create a competitive advantage. Being able to stand up work from home and virtual meetings for companies was a flexible strategy. Without it, they would have had to lay off thousands of employees as shelter in place orders impacted every industry. Those who were flexible and adaptable saw minimal disruption to their productivity.

Another top strategy for the last few decades, but especially this year is technology. Individuals and companies who can utilize technology can scale faster than most. Whether it's a new app, wearable, software program, smart device, or even just a new way of using technology like Microsoft Teams for school districts or physician visits with patients. Those that can invest, implement, and maximize technology continually put their competitors out of business (Netflix/Blockbuster example).

Along those same lines is an individual or company's ability to innovate. Innovation Strategy is finding new or creative ways of doing things to help companies to stay in business or reinvent themselves.

Apple for example moved from hardware to software to smartphones, tablets, watches, and no are getting into healthcare. A local grocery store in my hometown started using wagon-style robots to deliver groceries minimizing their need for delivery companies like FoodJets, Instacart, and DoorDash.

Similarly, utilizing data and knowledge to stay ahead of the market is known as the Information strategy. Individuals and Companies who can leverage data, research, and information can strategically plan years ahead of what their competitors can without those predictive analytics. One of the biggest pieces of data sold today is your social media choices and if you haven't seen the documentary released this year called *The Social Dilemma* - I highly recommend it.

The final competitive advantage strategy is Differentiation otherwise known as branding. When a company or individual can create a brand that penetrates a market, they can plant roots of loyalty with customers for years to come. Disney, McDonald's, Mercedes-Benz, Toyota, Samsung, Coca-Cola, Microsoft, Amazon, Google, and Apple were all the top ten brands last year whose combined brand value equaled $956 million. This was measured by their economic profit as well as the ability of the brand to create loyalty which becomes sustainable demand and profit for the future. Do you know what each of their brands is?

Recall Simon Sinek early and his decision to only do business with people who shared his values, this is part of a brand strategy. He shares a great example of the golden circle whereby the outer ring is what you have to offer, the second layer is how you differentiate from your competition, and the inner circle is why you are passionate or why you exist. According to Simon, "People don't buy what you do; they buy why you do it." So, do you know what your brand is? Individually or as a business? Why are people working with you? I can tell you why people are working with me, have hired me, and select me for recognition or awards.

I am *Fierce* - I live my purpose, values, strengths, and dreams with an intense passion for life.

Let me tell you about Madelyn. She is a young entrepreneur who has been ideating about a culinary business for a few years. At the start of the pandemic, she decided she finally had the idea and wanted to immediately launch it. As her coach, I suggested a little business planning first. She was so frustrated because her idea was to launch a homemade cookie and ice cream company with rotating specialty flavors and combinations not seen anywhere else in the area and June would be an amazing month to launch ice cream!

The first question I asked her was what you are going to sell it for, to which she responded, "I don't know yet." Madelyn had no idea how much supplies would cost her, the time and labor involved, the research planning and marketing needed nor what would differentiate her in this space. I asked her if this was something she wanted to do for fun or to make money and she said both. As frustrated as she was, I spent time going through each aspect of a business plan with her giving her questions to go research until a few months later she finally had it all mapped out.

Madelyn was right, there was no one in her immediate market doing homemade ice cream and cookies with a gourmet flavor twist. However, a franchise business had just come into the area south of us and had a similar business model. I asked her once more what would make her company different and this is when she came up with the membership concept. Unlike the new retail competitor nearby who would sell products individually, Madelyn wanted to sell her products as a packaged membership. A trio of three different featured ice cream flavors or a dozen cookies containing an assortment of that month's flavors. This allowed her to appeal to a market that would not have to choose just one flavor but could instead get a sample of all.

Once she had a pricing strategy for the memberships, had designed her marketing and branding materials, and had listed out all initial investment expenses, I reviewed her plan and committed to becoming her business manager. This story is about my daughter Grace Madelyn who launched her own business this past October at only 14 years old. You see, the tools I have shared with you throughout this book can be applied to young entrepreneurs like Grace, existing entrepreneurs like Abigail, or professionals like Caroline or Carolyne. Knowing your competitive advantage and the strategies needed to maintain it, are the final and critical steps to your *Fierce* strategy.

Glennon Doyle said, "once we feel, know, and dare to imagine more for ourselves, we cannot unfeel, unknow, or unimagine. There is no going back." Time to stand up and dance – you now have a *Fierce* strategy and all the tools and resources necessary to maintain it, refresh it, and go out and accomplish your goals. The final parts in **Exercise 6** may bring about questions, anxieties, or confusion and this is where my available consulting may be the right answer for you. Remember, I am available for a free thirty-minute call to review any of your needs and evaluate how I can help.

Strengths	Weaknesses

Opportunities	Threats

SWOT Example – Individual

Strengths

Strong work ethic

Loyal

Attention to Detail

Passionate

Ambitious

Weaknesses

Perfectionist

Easily Annoyed

Over-Commit

Opportunities

Finish Master's degree

Start Yoga and Meditation

Threats

Extensive Work Hours

Family Responsibilities

Community Responsibilities

SWOT Example – Business

Strengths

Product Quality

Employee Satisfaction

Niche Services

Weaknesses

Declining Revenues

Increasing Expenses

Opportunities

Technology app investment

Financial consulting

Threats

New start-up in the market

Sales Tax Increases

Competitive Advantage Exercise 6 – Part 2

7 Types of Strategy
Cost Strategy
Operational Strategy
Flexibility Strategy
Technology Strategy
Innovation Strategy
Information Strategy
Differentiation Strategy

Owning the Journey

"Passion + Strengths + Compassion = Purpose"

— Jay Shetty

Your *Fierce* strategy has come together. You are now intimately aware of your purpose, values, strengths, and dreams so the journey can be filled with an intense passion for life. It is important to remember that your strategy is simply the energy you have decided to put forth into the values and priorities you have chosen to work on. Only you decide what you value, only you decide what makes it to the top of your list, or who and what aligns to those values. Then and only then can you communicate those out, collaborate with others of like mind and spirit, and get creative with your plan.

The ability to remain competitive is critical to your survival and your *Fierceness*. The six C's of this strategic planning guide I hope have been easy to follow, easy to try, and ultimately something you set the intention to do.

The men and women I have quoted throughout this book are just some of the *Fierce* individuals whose examples I hope are inspiration to you as they were to me. As Sara Bareilles sings in her 2013 hit *Brave*, "Say what you want to say and let the words fall out, honestly, I want to see you be Brave." Take those five core values, their aligned responsibilities, your communication and collaboration goals, your new creative commitments, and your identified competitive advantage and send it to me on a poster or a board for the opportunity to have a one on one coaching session with me!

It is time to build our *Fierce* army and I want to see all the amazing individuals living their values and passion for life. Feel free to tag #yourfiercestrategy in all your new and amazing developments.

So, now what do you whisper to yourself? What do you believe to be true about you? Are you *Fierce*? I believe you are and now you are equipped with the right tools in your tool belt to embrace the power of owning your journey. I recognize one of the biggest challenges when you step out into that arena are the critics, but maybe it's not them you are worried about. In fact, as one of my coaches once said "it's the Itty-Bitty Shitty committee" in your own head that can hold you back from this Fierce life you are ready to lead.

Trust me we all have one, that voice that says, "who do you think you are" or "you're not worthy or good enough." My favorite musical artist of all time is Jessie J – I swear she wrote the soundtrack to my life – and she struggled with rising to fame and the criticism that came with doing something she loved. The song *Loud*, on her album *Sweet*

Talker, best describes this non-stop frustration - "You hate me when I'm up, you love me when I'm down, I'm so confused by the world, the world is so Loud."

How can you drown out that negative energy and fill your *Fierce* bucket? Brené would say you reserve seats for the critics like shame, scarcity, comparison, and that fourth person in your life (parent, teacher, boss, co-worker) you know who they are. You wave at them and say, "I see you; I hear you, but I am not interested in your feedback." Brené elaborates that we are hard wired for human connection and "when we stop caring what people think, we lose our capacity for connection; when we become defined by what people think, we lose our capacity to be vulnerable."

You do not want the hustle of trying to pull off 'I don't care what people think' so instead take off that armor and embrace your *Fierce* strategy.

The first step was picking up this book, the next is following the guide, and the last thing to do is find yourself a coach. Remember being *Fierce* is not a solo adventure. The lioness does not sit alone, the Beyhive is always close by, the march is filled with thousands. Time to embrace the *Fierce* within you; stop saying yes to everyone else and start saying yes to you!

Let's develop the next step for your career, business, or personal journey so you can make the next year even better than the last. I applaud you for investing in yourself and now I would like to help you not only put it into action but sustain your newfound passion for life!

For further tools, resources, and to inquire about individual, group, or business coaching please email yourfiercestrategy@gmail.com

----

Time to embrace the Fierce within you;

Stop saying yes to everyone else and

Start saying Yes to You!

About the Author

Amber Adams-Dixon-Campbell is a Corporate Strategy Director who specializes in process improvement methodology and has spent two decades in business operations. She has worked in the transportation, construction, and healthcare industries. As a debut author, she is passionate about coaching others to achieve their personal and professional goals.

Amber received her Bachelor of Arts from Earl Warren College at the University of California at San Diego, her Master of Business Administration from Isenberg School of Management at University of Massachusetts Amherst and is completing her Doctorate in Business Administration from the California School of Management and Leadership at Alliant International University.

Amber lives in Northern California and is a mother of three, philanthropist, and active healthcare leader who has spent her career mentoring, coaching, and developing others along their journey. She spends time helping high school students in the Central Valley learn these valuable skills as well because she knows investing in the future generation is the key to our success. At the time of this book release, Amber accepted her first Board of Directors roles for a National Association.

For more information or to inquire about her coaching program please email yourfiercestrategy@gmail.com

Acknowledgements

For providing Fierce inspiration – Jennifer

For providing coaching – Kim

For providing editing and support – Jason

For providing feedback and love – Stephanie

For providing mentorship and development – Richard

Thank you to all who made this book possible